PRAISE FOR THE RULES FOR WOMEN IN B...

"Finally—a playbook for women who are done sitting on the bench and ready to run the whole damn field. Reading it feels like coffee with your sharpest, funniest, most unapologetically successful friend—the one who hands you the ball, calls the play, and yells, 'Run!' before you can talk yourself out of it. Catherine Lang-Cline doesn't just explain the rules—she gives you the game plan, the pep talk, and the extra pair of cleats you didn't know you needed."
—*Stephanie Forbes, CEO of The Forbes Group*

"Any woman who wants to win in business AND life needs to read this book. Catherine speaks directly to and for the women out there who want to reach higher, but stumbles through a lack of confidence and know-how because they need someone to hand them the playbook to win the game. Enter Catherine Lang-Cline. This book is both informative and holistic. Catherine doesn't just talk platitudes—she lives them. Grab this book today."
—*Kate McKay, IFBB pro competitor, keynote speaker, and bestselling author*

"*The Rules of the Game for Women in Business* is a must-read for both aspiring leaders looking for a playbook to success and proven leaders in need of a pep talk. Catherine's straightforward approach and fantastic sense of humor make this an easy read. And even for those of us who hated gym class, the 'sportsball' framework proved to be both motivational and relatable!"
—*Dr. Melanie Corn, president of Columbus College of Art & Design*

"AMAZING! I can relate to the struggles of showing up in rooms where the rules weren't made for me. This book gave me a new language and a new mindset."
—*Claire Coder, founder & CEO of Aunt Flow; Forbes 30 Under 30; Tory Burch fellow*

"Every woman should read this book! Catherine Lang-Cline doesn't just tell us the rules; she teaches us how to rewrite them. This book left me fired up, focused, and fearless."
—*Casey Brown, founder of Boost Pricing and bestselling author of* Fearless Pricing

PRAISE FOR THE RULES OF THE GAME FOR WOMEN IN BUSINESS

"*The Rules of the Game for Women in Business* is an energizing, honest guide for any woman who's ever had to navigate leadership in a room not built for her. Catherine Lang-Cline doesn't just share the playbook, she teaches you how to run the plays—boldly and with purpose. Her blend of straight talk, strategy, and hard-earned wisdom resonates across sectors. This book doesn't ask us to fit into outdated systems. It gives us the tools to lead differently—and win. It's a powerful read for women ready to claim their space and shift the game."

—*Angela Meleca, founder of Meleca Creative Advisors*

"I thoroughly enjoyed *The Rules of the Game for Women in Business*. I read it straight through once I started. The rules apply to both men and women, though, and I hope it gains a diverse audience. I had the advantage of knowing Catherine for almost twenty years, and it is a story that lines up perfectly with the woman I know. I saw her grow into a supremely confident business leader over those years. If the rules are followed and become ingrained, the reader will benefit greatly. Not directly mentioned in the book is that these rules help someone become something that Catherine embodies; that is, people love being around her. When someone can accomplish that, doors will swing wide open."

—*Hugh Cathey, CEO and board member of Celerity; chairman and CEO of Chromocare*

"I've known Catherine Lang-Cline for years, and as a fellow businesswoman, I've had the great fortune of witnessing her authentic exuberance and generosity in action. As I read her book, I kept thinking this should be required reading for any woman who owns a business or participates in the business world. Catherine's engaging and relatable style—both in person and on the page—provides a clear roadmap for how to navigate the business world successfully. Reading this book, I had the recurring thought that if I had only had it as a resource when I was starting out, how much wiser and better equipped I would have been on my journey to building both my professional presence and my business."

—*Merry P. Korn, MSW, CEO of MPK Enterprise Holdings, Inc.; Ernst & Young EY Entrepreneurial Winning Women Award*

PRAISE FOR THE RULES OF THE GAME
FOR WOMEN IN BUSINESS

"This is THE playbook every woman needs to lead and live boldly. Relatable and approachable, Catherine's highly valuable rules are now out of her head and into your hands. Take them, run with them, and create your own success!"

—Amy Franko, founder & CEO of Amy Franko Associates

"Catherine Lang-Cline's *The Rules of the Game for Women in Business* is the ultimate playbook for women ready to lead with purpose and power. As a serial social entrepreneur, I found myself nodding, cheering, and even tearing up as Catherine masterfully blended strategy with soul. Her insights on mindset, self-worth, and legacy building are game changers. This book reminded me that showing up, speaking up, and owning our brilliance isn't just important; it's essential. If you're ready to win in business and life, this is your guide."

—Sheri Chaney Jones, serial social entrepreneur;
founder of Measurement Resources Company and SureImpact

"Whether contemplating entrepreneurship or already in a corporate role, women seeking guidance to advance their careers will benefit from reading this book. Catherine's firsthand experience in becoming a leader is honest and practical. The chapter about 'knowing your best position on the field' is one that I will bookmark and revisit often."

—Darci Congrove, managing partner of GBQ Partners, LLC

"Catherine coaches up her readers with this witty, down-to-earth playbook. Her voice is smart and relatable as she hands us a Rosetta Stone for decoding the sports metaphors, language, and team dynamics often leveraged in business. Drawing from her experiences moving up from the workforce minor leagues to the big leagues as a CEO, her insights are both practical and empowering. Whether you're new to the game or playing to win, this book is a valuable, engaging read."

—Stef Goldberg, senior partner & founder of GSD Execution Partners

The

RULES OF THE GAME

for

WOMEN IN BUSINESS

A Playbook to Become the Leader

Your Were Born to Be

CATHERINE LANG-CLINE

Story **BUILDERS** PRESS

Published by StoryBuilders Press

Hardcover: 979-8-89833-008-8
Paperback: 979-8-89833-007-1
eBook: 979-8-89833-009-5
Audiobook: 979-8-89833-010-1

This book is dedicated to my beautiful daughter. May she have the voice and the strength to do everything she has ever dreamed of.

It is also dedicated to my husband, Pete, who never doubted any of my crazy ideas and always believed that I could do anything that I wanted to do.

.

I also owe a big **THANK YOU** *to the champions that believed in me, pushed me farther, or were catalysts for change in my life: Kristen Harris, Fiona Mitchell, Darla King, Michelle Kerr, Stef Goldberg, Phil Black, Trey Humphreys, Tom Katzenmeyer, Don DePerro, Hugh Cathey, Kathleen Lach, Lawrence Lang III, and Cathie Cline. To everyone else I have crossed paths with, I am grateful that we met.*

CONTENTS

INTRODUCTION

*The only person who can stop you
from reaching your goals is you.*

**—Jackie Joyner-Kersee, one of the most decorated female athletes of all
time in track and field**

I f you are a woman who has become exhausted trying to get ahead, then this is the book for you.

Getting in the room and getting ahead in business can be a tricky code to crack because many of the rules were not written with women in mind. The language is different. Why? Because our male counterparts have been playing the game of business for a long time and by the rules they created. They created a lot of terms and practices, and a lot of them revolve around sports terminology. So, rather than trying to fight the system already in place, get in the game by understanding the language and the rules.

More and more women are involved in sports, so you are probably familiar with much of the language. This book is about applying it daily as you walk through your career—not just the terms but the swagger. So don't look at it as me questioning your genius, but rather us all jumping in and having fun in the game.

I'd like to introduce myself. As President and CEO of my company, I grew it into a multi-million dollar business, and after almost twenty years, I sold it. During that time frame, I picked up several honors and recognitions, which you can read in my bio later in the book.

My story isn't about luck. It is about figuring out how a quiet, confident person could learn how the game was played. In a world where only about 7 percent of women who own a business grow it to $1 million in revenue, and only 2 percent of women-owned businesses are sold, I was able to do both. I am in a tiny group of business owners, and with that history, I have gained a lot of experience I can share with you.

Throughout the book, I have added some of the most effective books from my career progression. These experiences and book suggestions can help you, too, because getting ahead, getting what you want, and getting recognized are not just about hustle; they are about knowing the rules of the game in business.

This book is not about emotion because business is not about emotion but rather about understanding the game, the rules, and the language. I began my career in the late '80s when pantyhose were still required. (Shoutout to my pantyhose-wearing, shoulder pad sisters, because the game was almost impossible back then!) I worked for about seventeen years in marketing and advertising and then created a business based on everything I learned along the way.

THE CURRENT SITUATION

Let's start by checking the scoreboard[1] because we need to understand where we stand. Women are a true underdog story. We deal with being underpaid, overlooked,

---

[1] *You know this one, but for those that don't, this is the large board for players and spectators to see the current score.*

overworked, and sexually harassed. We are also expected to have a work-life balance that includes caring for a house, children, and/or parents.

Women often encounter biases that can affect their personal growth and form doubts about their competence due to stereotypical assumptions about leadership styles. As a result, at the time of writing this book, only a little more than 10 percent of women were CEOs at Fortune 500 companies. Are we less capable or less informed of how this game is played?

There is the pay gap. On average, women still earn less than men for similar work. Industries, job roles, and locations can exacerbate this pay gap, and as a result, we run the risk of having less saved for retirement. We are conditioned to think that we should be thankful for whatever is offered to us, not ask for more, not negotiate our salaries, and not charge enough for the services or goods that we offer. Societal norms and cultural expectations can impose additional hurdles, such as pressure to conform to traditional gender roles or the challenge of being taken seriously in male-dominated industries. For the record, almost all industries are male-dominated.

These are all heavy-lift items, and the first step in equaling the playing field[2] is to acknowledge that almost all women have to face at least one of these things and that most situations can be course-corrected if we know what to do. There are some organizations that will simply not change, and those clients and companies don't deserve us, so we should move on as effectively as we can.

---

[2] *A field used for outdoor team games. Many of you have gotten hypothermia watching your children play on one of these.*

I have been in the business game for decades, and I would be remiss if I didn't give a nod to some of the ladies I learned from. Many of the women blazed the trail for the rest of us and, as a result, gave up everything to be in the game. It was my honor to watch them in action.

One thing I was very aware of was that many of these women were being taken advantage of, stabbed in the back, called bitches, and put in positions to fail. That frontline of defense[3] made it possible for the rest of us to play the game more fairly. Let's not just grab the ball from them; let's run with it. They had to practically dress like men, and definitely act like men, to even get in the room.

Because of their heavy lift, we get to play less aggressively and more strategically, and believe it or not, now many men welcome us to the conversation. That conversation only works if we speak up, use the same language, and know the rules because men are willing to be helpful when they know you are a great player on the team. They also want to move forward and make some money, and this book will help you run in the game like a champ.

WINNERS ARE ALL IN

Are you ready to win? We need more women willing to learn the rules and compete in the arena.[4] This book isn't about making you into something you are not; it teaches

---

[3] In sports like American football, the "front line of defense" refers to the defensive linemen, the players closest to the line of scrimmage, whose primary role is to stop the opposing team's running and passing attacks. Basically, they're the first people to take the hit.

[4] A large structure for open-air sports or entertainment. Nothing like a great arena concert, am I right?

you how it works. It will not make you a tyrant, but it will make you a great player.

Do you feel too nervous or unsure about stepping into the winner's circle?[5] Do not worry; everyone is an anxious mess when we do anything new or uncomfortable. This book will teach you how to be more comfortable with or thrive with that discomfort. We change those nervous bats flying in our stomachs into excited butterflies.

This book will also discuss impostor syndrome—where it comes from, how to get out of our heads, how to identify if the people around us are our cheerleaders or our cages, and much more.

Since men are more prevalent in business, especially in leadership roles, they use a lot of sports terminology that many women need to be made aware of and understand as fluently as their male counterparts. For this book, I will use many sports terms (watch for footnotes) and quotes to get you more comfortable communicating and understanding and, ultimately, more in the game. You may know many of the terms or all of them already, but this book will get you so comfortable with as many as possible that you'll be able to use them daily when communicating.

I will also explain the rules of the game to you. I'll be entirely upfront: it sometimes feels like you are walking into an all-male clubhouse, but if you play like a pro, you will be welcome into the group. Channel those times when you would hang out with your brothers or male friends. A considerable part of that "playing like a pro" is coming in with a winning mindset versus "everyone gets a trophy." You

---

[5] *The area where the winner of a game, contest, etc., receives his or her award.*

can be great at this. Your friends, family, and counterparts are all here and need you to accept the challenge, step up to the plate,[6] and receive your greatness.

Too sporty? Don't run away yet! Think for a minute. Who doesn't want a winning team? We all remember being on the playground, and people would pick teams, one by one, until the one last person, defeated, sulks over to the team that got stuck with them. That person is chosen last because the team captain doesn't believe they are a strong player or that they have enough confidence, and therefore cannot deliver a win.

Business is the same, and this book will walk you into that first or one-hundredth meeting and take you all the way to the boardroom if you are ready. It contains samples of scripts you can use to make better connections. Team leaders pick people who will help them win the game. If the only thing keeping you from being competitive is knowing the rules of the game, why not pick up the gauntlet?[7]

Do you feel frustrated or angry? Rather than direct that anger onto someone else, look at it as the catalyst for you to change and get more for your own life. Anger takes up a lot of thought and energy. We are going to redirect it into drive, determination, and fuel for change. We are going to turn your frustration or anger into strategy and figure out why we get pushed back, held back, or even worse, hold ourselves back. Our brains struggle when things are uncertain. This

---

[6] *In baseball, the plate, also known as home plate, is flat, five-sided, and marks the area where the batter stands and the base runner must touch to score a run. Check your hair; this is where all eyes will be on you.*

[7] *A gauntlet is a long glove worn for protection. Throwing down a gauntlet means someone is ready to compete. Picking up a gauntlet means accepting a challenge. You'll notice a lot of clothing and gear is thrown in sports.*

book will help you with that uncertainty by illustrating how much of it is actually predictable.

CHECKING THE EQUIPMENT BAG

This book contains everything I have picked up along the way over the last few decades. It is playing the long game.[8] I never considered myself competitive; my head mostly thought about it as digging in to get traction, not lose ground, get credit for what I did, and be either paid or acknowledged for it. I'll fully admit that my biggest competitor was myself, and it is probably the same for you. What helped is that I am curious and always love learning something new. It's like moving across a board, like a chess game, to capture the queen.[9] It was about working hard and winning. And why not? The best part is that you can still look good doing it.

I know you are a game-changer, and many women out here want to see you in the game, too, not just in the game but winning it and championing other women to do the same. We are winning it for our ancestors who fought the good fight and for those who follow us. We are winning it for ourselves, our financial security, satisfaction, and brilliance. From now on, we will start by not showing up for

---

[8] *"Playing the long game" means making choices and engaging in actions that, while they might not yield immediate results, are strategically designed to lead to long-term success and positive outcomes. If you lack patience, this is a tough one.*

[9] *The most powerful piece on the chess board, the queen, can move any direction across as many squares as needed in a move. Yaaaas Queen!*

a hockey game in cleats.[10] We will have the right equipment and knowledge of the rules to compete.

Women need to earn what they deserve and take advantage of all opportunities. It is so important to gather as much as we can from our careers because retirement comes fast, ageism is real, and we need these building blocks for our futures, our financial security, and our legacy.

Start now because five years, then ten years, will pass, regardless of whether we take action or not. Take some action, even a little, and get further than you are today. Regret is a real emotion, and we typically regret more things we didn't do than what we did and really messed up. You tried. You will not be perfect, but you need to try anyway.

Throughout history, women have been credited for some incredible feats because they were curious, created a vision, and tried. For example:

- *In New York in the '60s, Marie Van Brittan Brown created the first home security system.*
- *In the late 1800s, at the age of forty-five, an unemployed Josephine Cochrane invented the automatic dishwasher.*
- *The first self-made female billionaire in the United States was Martha Stewart.*
- *When she assumed leadership of* The Washington Post, *Katharine Graham was named the first female CEO of a Fortune 500 company.*

All of these women and so many more believed in themselves. They thought, "If not someone else, then why not me?" They went all in on something they were passionate

---

[10] *Those spiky things at the bottom of shoes for better traction on grass or artificial grass. You know when our stilettos sink into the ground? Yeah, like that.*

about that changed other people's lives for the better. They got in the game, no excuses, and got the job done.

I'm going to list a few excuses that I had starting out, and a few that I have heard others say. You may have more to add to the list, but if any of these are in your brain now or on repeat in your head, we are going to call them out now as the thoughts that slow us down.

- *I am afraid.*
- *I am too shy.*
- *I am too nervous.*
- *I don't have enough experience.*
- *I don't want to be greedy.*
- *I don't want to rock the boat.*
- *I don't have time.*
- *I don't know anyone who can help.*
- *I can't risk what I have made so far.*
- *I don't want more responsibility.*
- *I have too much on my plate.*
- *I don't deserve to be here.*
- *I have a huge responsibility to other people.*
- *I can't get out of my comfort zone.*
- *I don't want to get involved, I just want to observe.*
- *I don't think my opinion matters.*
- *I'm not smart enough.*
- *I will just leave the big decisions to other people.*
- *I am not enough.*

I see all of this, and I see you, and if you are ready to shake off these excuses, then you are prepared to win. Take all of the information I am giving you very seriously, and by that I mean, be willing to try it. Dig deep.[11]

HUDDLES, WHISTLES, AND QUOTES OF INSPIRATION

I am going to be telling you what to say in certain circumstances to crack the ice, to get you noticed, and to be more confident to reach the next level of your potential. This book has a lot of footnotes that contain the definition of all the sports terms I am using. It will also have HUDDLES,[12] which refers to an exercise, a moment of reflection, or a coaching moment. You will also see WHISTLE[13] sections, which are areas to pay attention to because I will share some vital wisdom. You will also see quotes from female athletes added in to inspire. These women had a mindset to win, and you can too.

Before you advance to the next chapter, let's start with a Huddle.

HUDDLE Take a moment to reflect on what winning means to you. Really define it with words or pictures. Make the vision so clear that you can practically walk into it right now. Think about the happiness you will feel, the change that will happen in your life and the lives

---

[11] *In cycling, the term "dig deep" refers to the practice of pushing through a difficult situation, usually in training or during a race.*

[12] *A quick conference before a play. Women don't call it this typically, because we are natural communicators.*

[13] *When a whistle is blown in sports, it means something important is happening, happened, is starting, or ending. It is basically a "listen up," this is important information.*

of your loved ones, and the things you can do as the payoff for working so hard. Think about abundance being all around you. Hold on to that feeling because it is your personal definition of what it means to be a winner.

Are you ready to learn the Rules of the Game? All hands in.
"Champions" on three... One... Two... Three...

CHAMPIONS!

RULE #1: YOU ARE HUMAN AND WE ALL START IN LITTLE LEAGUE[14]

You never know if you can actually do something against all odds until you actually do it.

—Abby Wambach, soccer player, coach, and
National Soccer Hall of Fame member

The first day of school. The awkwardness of high school. Finding your group in college or on the path to your career. The first day on a new job. It is all the same—we feel nervous, a bit lost, maybe a little nauseous.

I was the poor, weird art kid in high school trying to fit in. It didn't work. I tried to be funny, be overly pleasant,

---

[14] *The very first level of play, and baby, we all have to start somewhere.*

and help them on projects, but I could never make that big move of fitting in with the popular kids. They barely knew I existed.

In hindsight, it was a learning experience. It prepared me for walking into a business gathering, and no one knew I existed. The thing is, we all start at the beginning over and over again. It's how we grow and learn things along the way; we take notes because we will apply them going forward. This culmination of experience is the next level of growth mode; with that, you need a growth mindset. With a growth mindset, you can think beyond your current situation. We all have moments of thinking, "I will always be in this position." But we are never done growing. Three great examples of this are these women who changed their game after age fifty:

- *Hattie Caraway became a U.S. Senator.*
- *Toni Morrison became an award-winning novelist.*
- *Michelle Yeoh, at age sixty, received her first Academy Award.*

So you are still growing as long as you have breath inside you. Rather than thinking you are entering a situation as the weakest link, believe that you have gotten this far with this much. Get excited because you are where you need to be for what is next.

Every morning is a new day and a new start to the new you.

BE THE MAIN CHARACTER OF YOUR STORY

We all have a story that comes with our big bag of personal issues. For me, it started with a controlled upbringing and a constant struggle to fit in. I was raised in a religious household, led by my father. The expectation placed upon me was to marry a nice local Catholic boy and to work in the factory located in the neighboring town. This was a perfectly acceptable life, but it was not a future that ever felt right for me.

We were blue-collar, and life was more of a survival story than a growth story. As the oldest girl, I had significant responsibilities at a young age since my father worked the first shift and my mother the second shift. Taking care of my siblings was my most important task.

It was challenging even dreaming of better things. No one could help me with my oddball skill of being an artist. I had a wild imagination and a desire to learn and do better. My desire to find my right place in the world could have caused a big rift in my relationship with my immediate family. That gut instinct, that drive, led to a way out of that town, and because it was viewed as a life that I rejected, it caused some pain.

I had my sights set on college to explore the idea of having a career in art. Four and a half years later, I graduated and feared going back home, which led to a direct path into a dysfunctional marriage. I could have remained stuck there, but twelve years later, I took another big leap out of that situation with no regrets. I needed to walk through that fire to get where I am today.

The good news is that I am, and you are, right where we need to be, with all of our misfires, mistakes, damage, or brokenness. Add in the wins because all of it is a part of the learning and the journey, and it is everyone's story. Don't be ashamed of your story; it will make for excellent storytelling and inspire other people who are also finding their way.

If you are in a situation where you are the product of someone else's effect on you, know you can break free. I was raised by parents with five children to whom they paid little attention. I was married to the villain in my fairytale. I learned that I could not only be a better parent, but I could be my own hero.

Our origin story does not influence our careers as adults. All of my origin story may have made me scrappier, more self-sufficient, and a lot tougher. Knowing your ups and downs means you must speak to yourself with compassion. It also means that sometimes we can get where we need to go even if we are slightly broken. Think of yourself as kintsugi, the Japanese art of repairing pottery with gold, highlighting the history and imperfections of the repaired piece. We are all so shiny! And the best of the best in sports is also awarded in gold.[15]

Your parents may have been uninvolved, or they may have smothered you. You may have dodged a bad marriage, are in the middle of a challenging one, or have the best partner ever. Regardless of your circumstances, you are the main character in your story. You can blame others, you can make excuses, but the story you write for yourself is yours alone.

---

[15] *A gold medal signifies the highest achievement or victory in a particular contest or event.*

What you do and how you react to everything is under your control. You can blame a lack of sleep, addiction, or your current circumstances for holding you back, but it is only you that you can truly count on to make a change and get out of your circumstances. Or sometimes, we have to train ourselves and run that marathon[16] alone. Suppose running is not an analogy you can relate to. In that case, there are tons of other examples of sports that are done solo and that you can use as an example because in solo sports, people strive to achieve a personal best[17] with the hope of being better athletes.

Going solo, with a partner, or as a team can all get you where you need to go. For me, most of my life was that marathon, at least in the beginning. I have had falls and twisted ankles along the way, but the cadence[18] is rhythmic and constant.

In running, the cadence is the sound of your feet or the music in your ears that sets the pace. Rowers follow a cadence, and in order to go faster or be competitive, they have to increase the cadence. Think of the cadence and rhythm of your career. Is it set to a pace that gets you where you want to go? What are you doing to increase your cadence every day and advance yourself in business? You must get out of survival mode, change your behavior, and set your cadence.

---

[16] *A long-distance running race, strictly one of twenty-six miles and 385 yards. Truth be told, I've only achieved a half-marathon, and I think the training was everything I had in me genetically.*

[17] *The fastest time, highest score, best result, etc., that a particular person has ever achieved in a sporting event. Not every sport needs a team, but every sport is easier with people cheering us on.*

[18] *A measure of speed. In sports it can be defined as the number of steps, rows, cycles, per minute. The faster the cadence, the faster you go cha, cha, cha.*

Setting your cadence starts with defining your routine. Your daily routine might be:

- *Wake up.*
- *Make coffee.*
- *Do my makeup. hair. and pick out an outfit.*
- *Make my lunch.*
- *Drive to work.*
- *Do work things.*
- *Pick up the children.*
- *Have dinner.*
- *Do kids' things or start binge-watching something.*
- *Go to bed.*
- *Repeat.*

This is a perfectly fine, normal day. But the people who grow are the ones who start sneaking in one or two more things for the sole purpose of advancement. Let's look at that again, but with a few things added:

- *Wake up.*
- *Make coffee.*
- *Do my makeup. hair. and pick out an outfit.*
- *Make my lunch.* **NOPE! INSTEAD, go to an event, plan a lunch, and make connections.**
- *Drive to work.* **LISTEN to an inspiring podcast.**
- *Do work things.* **SEND two emails out to people that you want to connect with.**
- *Pick up the children.*
- *Have dinner.* **MAKE something you enjoy, and savor it.**
- *Do kids' things or start binge-watching something.* **MAKE either as fun as possible.**
- *Go to bed.*
- *Repeat.*

The idea is to make intentional little changes every day that will get you where you want to go. Change them up, add a few more, or steal time from binge-watching to do something productive. It can be something big or small; it just needs to be something to move you forward.

One of my favorite stories about cadence is Roald Amundsen's journey to reach the South Pole. Jim Collins even uses this example of the twenty-mile march in his book *Great by Choice*. The quick notes are that Amundsen and his team had a huge and challenging task. They committed to march toward the South Pole, regardless of the circumstances, to be the first to achieve it. They marched snow or shine. They didn't take days off when it seemed impossible. They marched knowing that if they did this same march every day, they would be successful and reach their goal. The Amundsen team survived and reached their goal, while their competitors perished.

To reach your goal, you need a cadence. Approach every day as an opportunity to take a step forward toward your goal, no excuses. Wake up and march. Mix up activities so you don't get bored; like a great gym workout, it shouldn't be "leg day"[19] every day. The people who get ahead are constantly strategizing their next step. If there is a dead end in one direction, they calculate a different direction or figure out a way around. There are no mistakes, only lessons to be applied. Plan, step, repeat.

Those steps can turn into big leaps. Keep score of every glimpse of movement to build your momentum. You may

---

[19] *Leg day refers to lower body exercises focused on a single day, typically as part of a body part or movement pattern training split. But girl, work out that whole body and brain all of the time.*

not be at your destination yet, but you saw a glimpse of it happening. You may have made the perfect presentation, been quoted in an article, raised your rates, shaken the hand of an influencer, or made the perfect hire. Little wins happen every day, and we need to acknowledge and celebrate them. When your head is focused on the cadence, you sometimes miss those little bits of growth, the glimpses that the plan is all taking shape. Capture the glimpses and acknowledge the glimmers of hope to see the seeds of success beginning to sprout.

The best leaders are constantly curious. They love learning new things as it triggers them to keep knowing more and improving. If you feel like that childhood wonder has fizzled out a bit, there are so many easy ways to reignite it. This can be achieved with:

- *Webinars*
- *YouTube how-tos*
- *Books*
- *Classes*
- *Conferences*
- *Panel discussions and presentations*

Start by reengaging with things that you were curious about when growing up. Maybe next you can be curious about a task that you have wanted to complete around your home. Then determine where you feel like you are falling short in business and educate yourself, little by little, in that area.

Learning does not stop after the diploma hits your hand—it is constant. And we have so much information at our fingertips that we can quickly stop watching that stranger's reel of them falling on a sidewalk and dedicate that time to something we can add to our cadence. If you feel that a person in your position should be doing more presentations, look into how you can improve them and who might be the group that wants to hear them. (A great book to attack your need to do the perfect presentation and step into your authenticity is by Karen Hough, *Be the Best Bad Presenter Ever.*)

The way to keep growing and fill the gaps you need to advance is to keep learning. Look into what you may need to know in order to graduate to the next level. School only takes us so far and primarily teaches us how to learn. It is up to us to take the baton[20] from there.

The people who ask questions, are open to curiosity, and constantly learn are the ones who get ahead because this is part of the practice[21] of business. Practice is vital to success, so we should try to do some form of practice daily. Our abs get better when we work out a few times a week. Our careers get better when we put in the work a few times a week. This is imperative because leaders and those who get ahead know that the landscape is constantly changing, and their behavior needs to change. So they must be prepared as people will look to them for guidance. Be ready.

---

[20] *In track and field or track events, a baton is a short stick that is passed from one runner to another in a relay race.*

[21] *In sports, practice is a structured activity that involves athletes working to improve their skills and performance. I mean, the first time we painted our nails on our own it was a mess. It only got better with practice.*

FAILURES ARE LESSONS FOR GROWTH

Some things to be aware of as you climb further are that it can get lonely out there, back to the solo sports. In leadership, and I'll paraphrase Shakespeare by saying, "Heavy is the head that wears the crown." By choosing leadership, you have to learn to be comfortable with additional responsibility, which includes duties that only you can execute and decisions that only you can make. And sometimes mistakes are made. You are entering a special club where only fellow leaders can understand what you are going through and where you all have common ground. It is lonely at the top because all the tough decisions are made there.

Next, not many other women will be in this club, but that is okay because you already have the leadership responsibility in common with everyone in the room. And these guys are just people; if it helps, you can recall what it is like to have brothers. If you didn't have brothers, you surely have been around guys, and the dynamic is the same. Some men like having women around, and some men are threatened. But the ball that you need to chase in this game is the one of commonality.

Both types of players typically identify themselves fairly quickly. Know your audience, and if possible, invite or elevate other women to be in the room, not for your comfort but simply because more women need to be in this room and they need to feel like they are invited to be there. Imposter syndrome is real and appears at the strangest times, especially when we don't know people in the room, if we know the people in the room are more accomplished than we are, or sometimes for reasons that we don't know.

Seeds are planted when we are very small children and by people we love who make us question ourselves. Sometimes we question ourselves for no reason other than "Why did I wear this jacket?" Not to worry, because everyone in the room has dealt with this on some level. Maybe the narcissist in the room hasn't, but more than likely, they are not looking to create great connections anyway. And everyone else in the room knows that about them.

Stay tuned for a great exercise to get those doubts out of our heads, but for now, know that you are capable of just about anything because you are the one writing your story. You are the main character of your story, and doing new things doesn't mean you are forever unqualified. You have learned a lot up until now—how to ride a bike, do math, drive a car, and almost all of your tech—and having the desire to do more new things is what is going to make you competitive. Every lesson learned gets you ready for your next step.

One of the biggest life lessons I faced was getting divorced. Simply said, divorce is like falling into a black hole, and you need to keep a daily march going and look for that glimpse of light to appear. I learned my value and what I wanted and didn't want. I learned those years were the fire I needed to walk through to get where I needed to go. That relationship was a twelve-year lesson that a new day can come at any time, because you keep your head up and look for it. What kept me in that place for twelve years was imposter syndrome and people-pleasing, thinking, "This is as much as I deserve or that I am capable of," and "I can't embarrass my family with a divorce," or "If I try harder, I can make him happy."

Letting go of relationships where you are not growing can begin your journey of growth. Consider it a trade[22] because the current player is no longer up for the job. Changing my inner narrative was the thing that got me out. The next step was to re-recognize my own brilliance because for years, I was told differently, began to believe it, and started to become my own bully. That self-deprecation takes hold in order to protect ourselves from failure: "If I believe that I can't do it, why even try?" But stepping forward will get us out of disappointment and fear and get us where we belong—back into the zone.[23]

Notice that I didn't describe that marriage as a failure. Did it fail? Yes. But I prefer to look at it as a lot of learning. I learned what I wanted and didn't want in a relationship. I learned that I deserved better. I learned that I could grow in a different direction. I learned that if I lost everything, I still had my brain and could build again. The learning happens when we get fired or quit a job. It happens when we work through addictions, heal from loss, have to fire someone, or feel completely lonely. Gather all of that knowledge, be grateful for it, and break free by making a change.

---

[22] *In professional sports within the United States and Canada, a trade is a sports league transaction between sports clubs involving the exchange of player rights from one team to another. Players are traded to build opportunities for players or the club. You might just be on the wrong team.*

[23] *"Being in the zone" or "flow state" refers to a mental state of total focus, immersion, and effortless performance where athletes are fully present and react instinctively, often transcending time and self-doubt. Superstar!*

WHISTLE! Some women will never reach the podium[24] because of their thoughts about money. Many women fear making more money than their spouses and parents and hold themselves back in order to avoid a skirmish[25] based on who has the most power in a relationship.

The definition of a good father or husband has always been a man who can take care of their family. That expectation extends to your wife or partner not moving into the role of breadwinner. Men are slowly becoming more comfortable with not being the only provider, but it still can be a sensitive topic. This sometimes extends to adult children dealing with fathers who always want to have the financial power in the family. Everyone else holds back. Women might keep their salary completely secret from a loved one in order to avoid conflict (and there are circumstances where that is not a bad idea, and separate bank accounts are always a great idea).

Successful women can face friction in relationships with partners, parents, and friends. Start by understanding your own relationship with money. Think about how your parents treated money and how you treat it as a result. Understand the emotions connected and how others can feel differently. Some people come from a family of savers, and others are spenders. Some families were always in survival mode, and others never gave money any thought. Determine

---

[24] In sports, a podium is a raised platform where winners stand to receive their awards, typically with three levels for first, second, and third place. Be the champion of your money.

[25] A "skirmish" typically refers to a brief, minor, or heated confrontation or argument, often between players or coaches, that doesn't escalate to a full-blown brawl or major incident.

if your relationship with money is a genuine fear or if it is imagined, that if you grow too much, make too much, the power will shift, and you will lose relationships.

The truth is, relationships can change, and women see things evolve, like going out with friends or family, being asked to always pick up the tab, being asked to share their wealth, and giving until it hurts. In many cases, we are happy to share our abundance, but there is a sting when it is expected. So do we stay quiet or celebrate with loved ones? We need to surround ourselves with people who love us and would also be proud of us and our growth. Be around people who are proud of you, but most of all, be proud of yourself. Grow for yourself.

When you start to get into the financial flow, you need to control your giving and think about the health of your financial situation because you never know what could happen. That means planning for emergencies and planning for your retirement. Statistically, many women work all of their lives and have nothing to show for it because they never saved or they gave it all away.

Come up with a cadence for saving. Don't give away money when you need to be looking out for yourself. If you immediately think this is selfish, know that you can help more people when you are in a healthy financial situation and not always in survival mode. Your overall health depends on your financial health too.

> **Move toward people who see what you are meant to be, want you to have the best life, and see the magic in you. Find your fans.[26]**

In any learning process, we need people around us who we can learn from, who are thrilled with our growth, who accept us as we are, and who support us or get out of our way. People are eager to say, "I accept you as you are," when discussing our flaws, but they also need to accept us as we are when we are driven, determined, and feeling our power.

My fast-growing career in advertising and marketing led to many relationship changes, but I visualized where I wanted to go and began the march. I mentally kept it as a solo sport for the most part because only I had the vision of where I wanted to go, and I hoped my support team would be along for the ride.

My parents' vision for me was to work at the same place they did. For them, it was a great job, and they viewed it as something to be desired. My first husband wanted to be the breadwinner and for me to be "the wife," which was something he grew up with and felt was the ultimate goal. While this could have been a path for me, it was really someone else's desires and goals, not mine.

"How could you not want this?" was a question asked of me, and one I asked myself. It is hard to disappoint others, but to stay on track with your vision, you sometimes must make big moves that step away from the vision others have for you. It is only a disservice to yourself if you don't at least try to get to the greatest version of you. If you don't try,

---

[26] *A sports fan is someone who has a strong interest, enthusiasm, or attachment to a specific sport, team, or athlete. They attend games or are watching them. Find your fans and be your biggest fan.*

you waste your time here on earth. If you don't try, you are wasting your talents. Bloom.

> **We love that they love the original you; let's hope that they love the future you too.**

PRACTICE WITH PURPOSE

We all have the power to overcome so many things. I mean, if we as women can make it through the entire day in some of the most uncomfortable shoes ever made, everything else is easy. It is a process, a step at a time. Think about soccer and football players as they start playing as children, miss goals and get hit over and over again, and then rise to the ranks of pro. We need to get comfortable with missing and striking out[27] because the attempts we make are not failures but rather more attempts to succeed. The cool thing is that there are always more times to be at bat,[28] and each time there is a possibility of a home run.[29] It's a numbers game, and the more often you make the attempt, the more chances you have to get better.

As you are conquering more challenges, know that the more we level up, the more learning occurs and stumbles will be made, and then the competition gets greater. My feelings about competitors were never based on anger, but

---

[27] *In baseball, a strikeout occurs when a batter is put out by a pitcher (the guy in the middle throwing the ball) throwing three strikes, either swinging or looking. It's frustrating every time, which makes the hits so fantastic.*

[28] *The time when it is your turn to try to hit the ball in a baseball game: In a nine-inning game, you might get four or five at bats. Basically, we get many, many chances to score.*

[29] *A fair hit that allows the batter to make a complete circuit of the bases without stopping and score a run. Celebrate those home runs!*

rather on how I could be better than they were. Really observe how your competitors do business; it is the same as when sports teams watch the old games of their competitors before they compete with them next. Observe their flaws and think about how you can do better. Figure out where you have the advantage. This is where your personal brand and your business brand can set you apart because if you are offering them the exact service that they need or want, you win because their perception of you, your reputation, and the words that are spoken about you before you enter the room are what close the deal. This is your brand speaking for you. More on that later.

WHISTLE! In every role you have, look at it as a chance to learn something new. Think of it as a part of your training, much like putting together a workout schedule at the gym, and in order to get fit, you need to work on different muscles. Realize that the more you know and the more experience you have, the more opportunities are revealed, and the more people will want you on their winning team.

Have you ever been in a situation where you are with a group of people and someone asks, "Does anyone know how to... ?" And it's you! You get to be the hero in that situation. Gain as much knowledge as possible in your area of specialty and then expand from there. If you want government contracts, talk to people who have them, ask about the process, and learn as much as you can to be a player. If you feel off track in what you need to know as a leader, ask other leaders

for advice, look for things to learn to open those
doors, and be relentless so you have the advantage.
It may feel like you should know everything, but
the truth is no one knows everything. But you
can work your connections and find people with
experience. Eventually, you have the expertise,
the leverage, and the ability to teach other people
who are just getting started.

> **Never underestimate how much others are willing
> to help you. You only need to ask.**

Ask questions about things you may not
understand. For example, when I worked for
large corporations, budgets were a big part of the
conversation. I learned as much as possible about
budgets in my department, which came in handy
later when I started a business. After I started
a business, I learned more from accountants,
bankers, and advisors.

Leaders keep learning; the ones who don't
do so stop growing and get lapped[30] because
everything keeps moving, updating, and going
faster, and the pros know to stay updated. Learn
things on your own if needed; never wait for
an invitation, and learn things at events from
the specialists who are there. The best time to
strategize your next move is when you are fully
comfortable with where you are right now. Build
on your momentum.

---

[30] *In any sort of race, "being lapped" means a competitor has been overtaken by another
competitor who has completed one or more full laps of the course, meaning the leader is
now a lap ahead.*

Because we need to really understand this game we are playing a little deeper, here are a few not-so-fun facts:

- *More American women than ever are unmarried. In olden times, we would have called this woman a "spinster," which is a definition and often derogatory term for an unmarried woman past the age when women typically marry. The word originates from the Middle Ages when women commonly spun wool for a living. Because this was a job usually performed by unmarried women, the term came to refer to a single woman, even in legal documents. These women made their own money and did not have to rely on a man to marry them for survival.*

- *Before 1900, women could not own or inherit property in America. If they married, all their assets went to their husbands. Sorry if you didn't choose wisely when picking a spouse. If you left, you lost everything.*

- *Women were prohibited from obtaining credit until 1974 when the Equal Credit Opportunity Act was signed. Many women could not start a business without a man signing for the loan, even if that man was their eighteen-year-old son. Absolutely no credit cards were allowed in a woman's name (but I think that many retailers were a bit thrilled when all of that changed).*

- *When women first started appearing in office settings, they were paid less. This was determined because they didn't have a family to provide for or because they were not worth investing in since they would be leaving their careers to get married. At that same time, in business, if a man's wife was expecting, he got a raise to help provide for his family. If a working woman was expecting, she was let go.*

- *Statistically, almost half of Americans—about the same number of men and women—don't believe a woman can do as good a job as a man in leadership.*

The history of business shows that women have made huge strides but still make less and rise less because the playing field is not even. Women are treated less than because they are not seen as equals, and sometimes we let it happen. The odds may be against us, but we owe it to our ancestors not to give up any ground and to shoot higher.

Let's think about Martha Stewart, Oprah Winfrey, Sarah Blakley, Taylor Swift, and Beyoncé and the odds they would reach as far as they did. Taylor started in tiny venues. Oprah started on *A.M. Chicago*. And like the others, they kept marching forward against the stats and against the odds. Martha and Oprah both built brands that became empires. They are people like you and me, and they dug deep. They put on their game face[31] and played the game. They took the shots[32] people didn't think they had.

You can play the game too. These women were not given an advantage, but they did have drive and a few people behind the scenes who supported them. It is a formula. It is a strategy. All of this effort you have been putting in is useless without that same kind of vision and strategy. And you need to know the terms and actions in business—the rules and stakes—so you are no longer the last person picked to be on the team and ready to play the game. You walk on the field because you know that you belong there.

---

[31] *The face players make when they know they are going to have to try to do something exceptional.*

[32] *To propel a ball or puck toward the goal in order to score.*

It's worth mentioning that not everyone will achieve this epic status. I have not reached epic status like the women I just mentioned. But anywhere between where I am now and epic is worth putting a plan together. Am I right?

WHISTLE! Almost always, people in business cheer on the champions, male or female. I've witnessed it and, with hard work, advanced my career. Do not think for a minute that this is an "us against them" situation. Everyone earns their place at the table. It's about being the best. Ladies, it is time to see that we are equal and decide to go pro. [33]

HUDDLE Take a moment and think about the good and the bad about past relationships, and answer these questions:

1. Regardless of how you were raised, what gifts were you given at birth that make you a talented, strong, independent person?

2. Regardless of your circumstances growing up, what skills did you pick up in the game of life?

3. What do you wish you could have received from a bad relationship?

4. Was there a time when you were afraid to speak up? When did you "find your voice"?

---

[33] *Becoming professional in a sport or activity. And it is not about being good enough; it is about keeping the momentum going until we peak.*

5. Was there ever a time when someone
    made you feel "less than, powerless, or
    weak?" What did you do to change the
    circumstances?

A good therapist will tell you that "your
parents (or really anyone) did the best they could
with what they had." Whether you believe that or
not, that is the past. We can't change it, but we can
learn from it. And we can put all that we learn
to use—consider it the training needed to get
you where you need to go. All athletes need years
of training and prep before finding their stride.
You need to always be preparing, observing, and
learning for the next level of you.

Next, pick someone you admire. Think big.
When I was asked over twenty years ago, I chose
Martha Stewart. She built an empire in a man's
world; she became the first female with a billion-
dollar business. She is a brand and not known for
just one thing. She got where she is by playing the
game and being relentless, driven, strategic, and
at least outwardly, fearless. These are the things
that can move the needle.

Now you.

1. Who in the entire world would you pin
    to your wall and use as a guide to get
    you where you want to go?
2. What characteristics do you see in
    that person you want to bring out in
    yourself?
3. What disciplines did they have to get
    where they are?

4. What steps did they take to keep their
    momentum going?

Why start this now? Because there is time. "Future You"
needs you to take action now and get off the bench. When
you choose to sit out, you miss all of the opportunities and
all of the joy, and you make less money and save less money.
Be a beast now because aging is waiting for us all, and you
need to put yourself in the best financial position possible
to thrive.

Less than half of the women out here are preparing for
retirement or have any money saved. Many women don't
earn enough to save. For our survival, we need to turn the
tide. It is time to call our own audible[34] and change course.
We always allow ourselves to have conversations about
having a healthy body and mind. Still, we should also note
that having money and relieving the stress of always being
in survival mode is also healthy.

HUDDLE One of my favorite
exercises, which many
business coaches use, involves storytelling. It
is the story that we tell about ourselves. It all
starts with what you consider your "origin story,"
the story of your humble beginnings that you
tell yourself and others about who you are.
    What I would like you to do first is to
write your origin story. Write about how you
started out, where you lived, and how you were

---

[34] In American football when the quarterback changes the play at the last minute. The
quarterback is the one in control of the ball at the beginning of the play. You are in charge of
your own plays.

raised. Write about any wins or anything that was devastating. Add a few activities that you enjoyed as a child, the fun things, the things you did before you had big responsibilities. When finished, read it out loud to yourself.

Next, we write your story arc. This is the story that builds from your youth to where you are now. Write about the accomplishments, the hurdles[35] you jumped over, and each advancement in your career. Give yourself credit for absolutely everything it took to get to where you are right now. Read that story out loud to the child that you once were.

Take a minute to bask in your own story up until now. Really appreciate yourself for what you have accomplished to get here. Reflect on how twelve-year-old you would be impressed with how far you have come and what challenges you faced along the way.

One more step. You will write from your perspective of yourself, ten years from now. Same idea, but you will visualize where you will be in the next ten years. You have already overcome a lot; think about what you would still like to accomplish. Visualize it without thinking about how you might get there and write it down. Do you see yourself with a shorter work week, maybe traveling for a month or living somewhere else entirely? Understand that the superpowers you were gifted in your origin story are where it all started. Bear in mind, I am not talking about bending steel with your bare hands; these are

---

[35] *Essentially an obstacle that athletes leap over while running. Hurdles are so frustrating. Whether you make it over those obstacles or not, keep moving forward. Plan your course around it or keep practicing to clear it.*

simply the skills that you are fantastic at. Read that story out loud to the person that you are today.

If you are unsure, modest, or want to dig more into your superpowers, Mark Henson has written the book *Ordinary Superpowers: Unleash the Full Potential of Your Most Natural Talents*. You can learn that what comes naturally to you is actually extraordinary.

What advice would you give yourself today from that future perspective, from the storyline where you got the life you dreamed about? What would "future you" say to you? Would it be "keep going," "stop doing that," "take the chance," or "you are going to be so happy that you did that"? Write those things down and put them where you can see them often. Maybe get a saying engraved on some jewelry so you always have your "pep talk" with you.

With this life story you have written, you know what your gifts are and what you have accomplished, and you have a map of where you are going. Or it's like having all of the ingredients for a recipe. It's perfect timing to put together a playbook.[36]

---

[36] *A notebook containing descriptions of all of the plays and strategies used by a team. Start thinking about your next move, your next play to win.*

RULE #2: SHOWING UP AND PARTICIPATING BUILDS MOMENTUM

You make your own luck. You make it in training.

—Simone Biles, the most decorated gymnast in history, is regarded as one of the greatest Olympians of all time

Although I believed I had done all the homework, people still questioned my ability. Some people said, "You got lucky."

People will make a thousand judgments about how a woman got ahead, including other women. But the truth is that women train for advancement daily. It sometimes happens in the smallest of ways because no one is around to help. Every day, it is a choice to learn something, try something new, and invest in their career in some small way. It is not luck. It is showing up, being prepared, and being ready to get in the game; these are the three best things that you can do for your career. When you are ready, you advance.

> **You need to prepare for your next opportunity because the next opportunity will not wait for you to be prepared.**

You will be underestimated. We all are. If you enter the room as a woman, strike one. If you enter a room and no one knows you, strike two. But you can always keep it from getting to strike three because you always show up prepared. You come to play the game. Participate, generate ideas, give opinions, and volunteer to help with projects. Preparation makes a great team player, and everyone wants great players on their team.

I keep saying to "be prepared," but it may resonate more if I instead say, "be prepared for anything." Call it intuition, gut instinct, or "spidey-sense," but women always seem ready for what can go wrong. So when I say "be prepared," it means to be ready to react to whatever is thrown at you. Consider this checklist your "preparedness kit" for your next meeting.

- *Paper and pen. You can use a small notebook, but be prepared to take notes physically. Write down anything you need to remember. This could include important names or ideas you want to bring up but need to wait for the right time. The idea is to have your thoughts ready. You can take notes on your phone if you forgot your pen and/or notebook, but the perception isn't good, as it doesn't look like you are paying attention.*

- *Sit or stand in a place where you are near the presenter or the important players in the room.* You need to be seen over and over again by the decision-makers and game-changers. You want to be one of them. This is not the time to hide. Standing and sitting near the action means that you are ready to be called into the game.[37]

- *Listen with intent.* Getting caught up in a sidebar conversation or quickly replying to an email on your phone is an easy trap to fall into. Resist the urge and be present. People pay attention to the people who are paying attention. Plus, you won't get beaned by a ball.[38]

- *Know that someone is going to steal the ball*[39] *from you.* Be ready to steal it back. In other words, people will interrupt you, or they might try to steal your idea. Is it rude? Technically, yes, but in any sport, the person with the ball gets all the attention. The person who has the ball is the one who has the opportunity to score. Get the ball back so you can score.[40] Women have better tactics and finesse when the conversation is going at a steady pace. Men do not mind interruptions, but just don't sound like their ex-wife when you do it. Stop reminding them that it is your turn to speak. There are no "turns," and they know they have interrupted you. Dive into that conversation and get what you want.

- *Thank the presenters or the people conducting the meeting.* A lot of work is put into events and meetings, so your appreciation is appreciated, even a simple "Thank you for your time today" or "That talk was fantastic."

---

[37] In sports, being called into the game means being selected to participate in the game. Yes! We have been waiting for this.

[38] "Beanball" is a colloquialism used in baseball for a ball thrown at an opposing player with the intention of striking them to cause harm. Remember when our teachers would ask us questions when they knew we were not paying attention? Same thing.

[39] Taking the ball from your opponent. Men interrupt each other, steal ideas from each other, and try to look good to the group.

[40] To get a point.

I have waited and lurked numerous times just for that one statement. The results range from a quick brush-off to scheduling a meeting to talk later. Showing your appreciation makes a stronger connection that would never happen if you chose to do nothing. Give it a shot and try a handshake or a thank you. So easy. You just made someone's day, and as Maya Angelou famously pointed out, "I've learned that people will forget what you said, people will forget what you did, but people will never forget how you made them feel."

To learn more and advance, you need to be curious. Consider "How can I do it?" rather than "Should I do it?"

PLAY THE GAME LIKE THEY DO

Let's talk a bit about getting the ball back. Being interrupted may be the hardest flex for women because we are taught to be polite, to wait our turn, not to interrupt others, and to play fair. But if you watch any sport, players kick, scratch, and fall down to get the ball for their team to get possession or score.

While meetings don't actually get that physical, paint that picture in your mind and get mentally prepared. Know that for the most part, meeting participants see what transpires if someone is constantly interrupting or stealing ideas, but not always. That is because men are in that "team" mindset, and it doesn't matter who scores as long as they win. But women need to be seen as the star versus the person always doing the assist.[41] Here are a few things that you can try that have worked for me to "get the ball back":

- *Let them finish their statement, and then finish your thought. "Yes! Like I was saying..."*
- *"Okay, let me finish this thought before we get too far away from the topic."*
- *"I'm going to build on what was just said."*

You are not being combative, but this is how you can respond to the other person stealing your shine. Give their comments or ideas the same consideration that you would want yours to be given, and then make your presence and your ideas known. Sometimes, an idea that you stated earlier gets repurposed, and someone else gets the credit. Maybe you didn't say it loud enough. Perhaps the conversation was not ready for your brilliant idea. Maybe you were silent and someone produced the same idea that you were thinking, but once it is out and communicated, it is a fair ball.[42] Your next move is to go after it. Determine if it needs to be your win or the team's win. If you know that you clearly revealed a great idea first, for example, you can say:

- *"You don't have to convince me of this decision; I was already on board."*
- *"Great, my idea is still alive."*
- *"Now that my idea is back on the table, let's discuss the steps to implement it."*

If you were just thinking it or only had a start of an idea that someone else is now building on, all is not lost. Keep

---

[41] *The person that is always passing to the player that gets to do the actual scoring in a game.*

[42] *A batted baseball that lands within the foul lines; the ball is live and in play.*

building on it, ask clarifying questions, and show some enthusiasm around it, and the result will be that you are a great team player.

Does interrupting and being scrappy feel rude? Maybe. I just call it throwing elbows.[43] The bottom line is that you need to determine what works for you. The idea is to get possession of the ball[44] and know that this is how the game is played. It is expected. Rugby players are not courteous; they work toward a scrum.[45] American football players cause fouls[46] throughout the game, sometimes strategically.

Don't be scared; most meetings and situations are very amicable. Just always be on guard for someone's overzealous maneuver. Remember again that the team is here to win, but everyone wants to be the MVP.[47] You may be the one who assists or scores, but either way, good sportsmanlike conduct is what wins the day.

At some point, someone will be a complete jerk. It happens. Keep up the good conduct. I follow the rule of "three strikes and you are out"[48] concept. Be a good team member three times, and hopefully, it will redirect the other person to do the same.

---

[43] *"Throwing elbows" refers to using the elbows to push, shove, or hit an opponent, because we gotta get that ball back, baby!*

[44] *In sports, "possession of the ball" refers to a team's or player's control of the ball, granting them the opportunity to score or advance the play. Playing any part of the scoring is a win for you.*

[45] *Scrum is a means of restarting play after a stoppage caused by a minor infringement of the laws.*

[46] *A foul is an inappropriate or unfair act by a player as deemed by a referee, usually violating the rules of the sport or game.*

[47] *MVP = Most Valuable Player. And who doesn't want to feel valued?*

[48] *In baseball, the hitter at home plate will get many opportunities to swing at the ball, but if the pitch is good, it is considered a strike. After three strikes, the hitter's turn is done. At this point it is about exhibiting that you will be respected on this team.*

After that, the gloves are off,[49] and it is time to ask for some clarification in a controlled, direct way:

- *"Can you tell me why you are so angry/defensive/ upset right now?"*
- *"Do you not like my idea or me personally?"*
- *"I don't know what I said to upset you, but know it was not my intent."*

People get hostile because they feel like they are not being heard or are being made to feel small. Don't let that happen to anyone in the room. If the conversation gets challenging, let the other person know that you hear them, you understand them, and you appreciate their opinion. However, you are allowed the same courtesy.

Do not hesitate to share your ideas. Many women will sit quietly or fear interrupting, and the idea will come to someone else, and their only tactic at that point is to build on it. Get off the bench.[50] What you can do is say immediately, "I was thinking the same thing" to be seen as a fellow idea person, but whoever says it first is typically the winner of the idea.

Everyone is there to contribute; that is why you were included in the meeting. Might you spout off a terrible idea? Maybe. But what if it isn't? What if it ends up being the most awesome assist to someone building on your idea?

Be the idea person. A lot of businesses struggle because of the lack of ideas and new ways to do things.

---

[49] *A saying for when people or groups are ready to fight, argue, compete, etc. Gauntlets, gloves, hats, men are constantly throwing equipment about.*

[50] *In sports, "the bench" refers to the area where substitute players, also known as bench players, backups, or reserves, sit, waiting to be called into the game. Lean forward and be ready to go. Nothing happens here.*

If you are still afraid to shout out an idea, try presenting like this:

- *"I am not sure if anyone has thought about this before, but ..."*
- *"This might be a crazy idea, but I want to see if someone can build on this."*
- *"Based on my experience, have you thought about ..."*
- *"Would there be any reason not to try to ..."*

Do not be the one to sabotage your own ideas by saying something like:

- *"This might be a dumb thought, but what about ..."*
- *"I don't know anything about this, but ..."*
- *"I have this idea, but what do I know ..."*

Stop it. You are strong, educated, and experienced.

The new members in a group of CEOs who are really familiar with each other may struggle to get into the game. Just keep playing the game. They need to see if you are bringing value or if you have what it takes to be in the room. Spoiler alert: You do have what it takes.

From now on, consider yourself in training for a higher level of yourself. You are absolutely ready to get into the circles you didn't think you were fit for. Your solid values and behaviors are a great foundation; the rest is just gaining experience. Speaking up in meetings takes practice too. Everyone at a higher level knows more than those at the lower levels. Like a game, the better we get, the higher we rank.

THE FIVE Cs

You have learned so much up to this point, and everything you've learned can be applied to where you want to go next. Everything mentioned is the exact skills that will get you in the room and recognized.

Here are five of the top skills that served me well and that you should focus on to move forward and move the needle. I call them the Five Cs.

COMPASSION

The person with the loudest voice in the room and the one with the smallest voice both want to be heard. If you deal with every person in the room with that attitude, you begin your evolution onto the higher-level playing field. You may think the meanest, most boisterous, most obnoxious person gets to control the room, and they do try, but the ones who operate with the team mentality are the ones who get the respect.

To achieve this, you treat everyone as if they are your best teammate, and you want them to score. Can you curse their name as you walk away because they are a lousy team player? Of course you can. But it is "game on"[51] during meeting time, and we listen, pause, and conduct ourselves at a higher level. You might think that I am asking you to

---

[51] *"Game on" is an informal expression that means you're ready for a challenge or competition. This is the absolute fun part.*

get steamrolled,[52] but I am not. If someone tries to control a situation, you stand your ground and only speak to the facts.

- *"Here is what I know about the situation."*
- *"I know that you are excited about this, but you interrupted me before I could finish."*
- *"Let's review the facts so I understand."*

Keep it straightforward and even-toned, no shaming allowed, because people will push back if you try it, and you need to cut it off quickly if someone is trying to shame you. No one wants to be humiliated, so don't do it, and don't let them do it to you. That is not fair play. Also, look out for other team members who are struggling and make sure that they are heard. Actions like this will make you a superstar.

This will pay off. It exhibits you as a leader and makes people you thought were your enemies your allies and your allies your champions, and shows that you can navigate any situation. Compassion is not a weakness; it is identifying and alleviating a weakness. It is understanding where everyone is coming from and operating with a strategy that allows you to get the best out of them, or at least what you want to get out of them in general.

CURIOSITY

Be curious about everything. Do not be shy to ask questions. Curiosity and asking questions are the processes that keep us learning, and to stay ahead, you want to learn as much as you can.

---

[52] *Being completely overpowered and dominated by an opponent.*

Curiosity also means listening to the knowledge and experiences of others. The details for everything you need to know may be coming out of someone else's mouth. Listen and gather all that information before you utter a word, because someone else in the room may know even more than you do. Listening allows you to determine how informed that person is, their way of doing business, and how they want to be communicated with. Don't step back from fear; ask this person more questions, especially the ones no one else is asking, and learn more. Much like in football, no one moves until the quarterback gets the ball. Everyone waits and listens to the calls[53] because everything they need to know will be in those calls. Once the handoff is made or information is given, everyone adjusts in response.

Curiosity is learning as much as possible, and where better to learn than from your fellow CEOs and peers. It is not about feeling like the least informed person in the room because you cannot know absolutely everything; you know the things that are in your wheelhouse.[54]

Learn beyond the room you are in. As much as you can, be aware of trends in business and marketing, data results, and tech advances, and keep apprised of what everyone else in business is doing, especially in areas that you are in or wish to be in. Subscribe to blogs, podcasts, and business updates to at least be aware of what is happening. You don't need to overwhelm yourself; a little at a time is fine.

---

[53] *The specific play that a coach selects for the offense to run, which is communicated to the players on the field through a coded language, usually including formations, routes, and blocking assignments, depending on the situation in the game.*

[54] *In baseball, if a pitcher throws the ball in a batter's wheelhouse, they throw the ball to a place where the batter can hit it powerfully. Watch for that moment and swing!*

If you find yourself in a situation where you did not know about something and everyone else did, make a note to look it up later or ask for clarification if it feels like the right circumstance. People love to feel smart, so let them.

Speaking of other people, being curious about others is the best way to build relationships. You might think the best strategy is to tell other people about yourself first, but it is not. Get to know other people, such as where they work, how they got into their line of work, why they started a business, etc. Listen for connections. Maybe you went to the same school, know some of the same people, have a similar hobby, and the conversation takes off from there. Being curious at an event is the easiest way to make friends in a room full of people you don't know.

COMMUNICATION

Being very clear with your thoughts is key. We have all seen the person, or fear that we are the person, who stumbles with what they want to say. Or the person who rambles on too long or goes on thinking they are explaining something, and it goes over everyone's head. (Fun fact: When I was in marketing, all communication had to be at a fourth-grade level in order for the general public to understand it.)

Of course, you will be running with a much more educated group than fourth graders, but keep this in mind as people talk at the general level so everyone can feel included. If you are at an event and you are sharing information at a level that is way over their heads, not only is it wasted time for everyone, but the people listening to you are just made to feel ignorant—and we definitely don't want that.

Start simple and clear; think of it as an easy throw-in[55] or toss. If you discover that everyone understands what you do, elevate the conversation to match the group.

Always try to be very clear in storytelling, explanations, or ideas. If communication breaks down or is ill-received, it is your job to build the bridge back. If that happens, try saying:

- *"It is a little complicated; let me clarify."*
- *"My comment was not meant to offend but rather ..."*
- *"If you misunderstood, that is my fault; I sometimes get caught up in the jargon."*

COLLABORATION

You can either run alone or run with a team, and I can tell you right now that a team will get you farther because it allows you access to more talent. Other people know the people that you need to know and can help you with a really big leap. Collaborating with people—the right people—gets more done because everyone is offering their best skill sets. Best of all, when collaborating with others, they see how you work and how reliable you are, and they will recommend you for bigger and better things.

Working with others and letting them see what I could do led to recommendations for board positions and opportunities to be in the room where big decisions were being made, and it will lead to recommendations for you.

---

[55] *An easy throw, often used to put the ball back in play or to a teammate, is commonly called a "throw-in."*

People want people in the room because they are reliable, relatable, collaborative, and honest, and most of all, they show up and deliver.

Good collaboration can open doors that you didn't know existed. The last thing you should do is underestimate your worth in those situations because you probably have the skills they need, and if you say "no," you miss your opportunity to be a part of something bigger.

You also have to be selective. Knowing that you can contribute to something should not be one-sided, so ask yourself these questions:

Why does someone think that you would be a great addition to their team?

- *Is it something that you are great at and love to do?*
- *Would it get you in the room with a new group of champions?*
- *Is it a position where you would gain valuable experience?*
- *What would a "yes" to a collaboration mean to you in the long run?[56] Determine if it is worth saying "no" to other things.*

You only have so much time in your day to determine if this will be a great investment. With that said, there are endless volunteer opportunities, so choose wisely. Better yet, pick an organization you would like to volunteer with and ask if they have an opening on a committee or on their board. That way, you can learn and contribute to a purpose that you believe in at the same time.

---

[56] *The overall outcome or benefit over time that comes from building endurance and consistent performance.*

COURAGE

At some point, you will have to be bold. You will have to embrace your courageous spirit and go after what you want. You may think this is not your personality, but I am willing to bet that there was a time, maybe even when you were a child, when you saw something you wanted and figured out a way to get it.

We have experienced courage at times when we didn't think we had it. One of my first experiences was getting myself into college. My parents were not on board with the idea of my leaving town, and they didn't go to college themselves, so it was completely uncharted territory. My situation at the time of this decision was that I was in charge of my siblings when my parents were at work, including laundry and making meals. My courage had to be initiated when it came to disappointing my parents and dropping all of that responsibility and moving away. Courage is when you face your fears and do the brave thing anyway.

My parents were also not in a financial position to send any of their five children to college, so I had to find the money. I had to be bold, research colleges alone, go to banks for loans, pack my things, and leave my home. I did what I needed to do and made it happen because I felt that it was right.

We have other relatable circumstances where we had to find the courage to make things happen, like asking out the guy we like, approaching the celebrity we want to meet at an event, asking for a raise, quitting a job, and facing fears in other ways. You might not know how it will work out, but even if it fails, at least you tried. Most regret comes from never trying, not from trying and failing.

It is daring to dream bigger for yourself and plot a course to get everything you need, want, and can't imagine having. It could be quitting the people who are holding you back or finally starting a business. It is deciding that you deserve better and continuously conjuring ways to get there.

GET CREDIT FOR WHAT YOU CAN CONTRIBUTE

We often sell ourselves short on some of the most important experiences that can contribute to our growth. For example, you know that you are a "get it done" person if you are the one parent who can always deliver the juice boxes on time to a sporting event, or you make the presentation happen for the next day after someone just informed you of it at 4:00 p.m. If you are the person who can organize a kitchen or a dinner better than everyone else, you are a project manager. If you are the one sending out all of the correspondence from the family, talking to the doctor for a loved one, or always the peacemaker among family and friends, then you have great communication skills. Skills like these can be redirected from your personal life to your business life. Take credit for all of it and apply some of this time and energy to your own advancement.

Repeat and practice everything you have learned in your daily activities. Strengthen your bio with the knowledge you gain in every book you read, class you take, experience you get involved in, and everything you try, and then keep adding more to what you already know. Look for things you want to know, figure out what you need to know, and start plotting and stealing time to get this commitment to yourself done.

The best wins happen when everyone participates to the best of their abilities and brings their best game. Are you showing up as a team player, undistracted, and all-in? Or are you phoning it in? Are you always on your phone? Pay attention and keep your eye on the ball.[57] The twenty minutes you are scrolling on your phone, you could be doing something far more productive to advance your career. You are stealing time from yourself.

Show up and participate. If you attend a meeting and say nothing, you run the risk of not being asked back. Saying and doing nothing or not investing in the time there will eliminate you from being invited to join the bigger leaders. This may be a big lift for those who consider themselves introverts, but you can do this. You need to have a G.O.A.L.

---

[57] *Basically, pay attention. Everything happens around that ball and you have to be ready to react.*

SCORING A GOAL IN NETWORKING

What is the G.O.A.L.?
- **Grit** *to show up*
- **Own** *your voice*
- **Act** *with courage*
- **Leave** *with lasting connections*

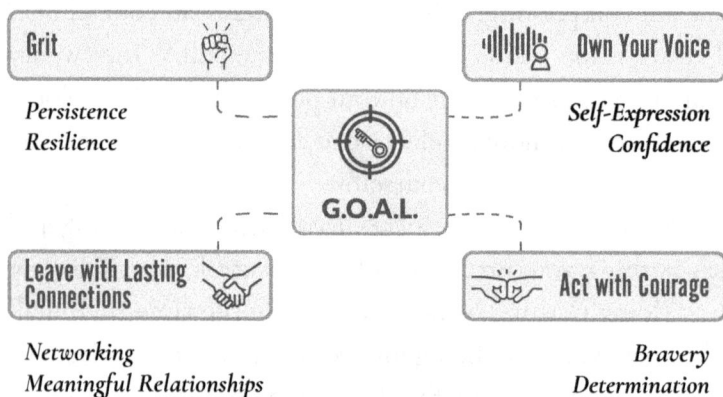

Grit		Own Your Voice

Persistence
Resilience

G.O.A.L.

Self-Expression
Confidence

Leave with Lasting Connections   **Act with Courage**

Networking
Meaningful Relationships

Bravery
Determination

GRIT TO SHOW UP

You are here. This is a big deal because so many people find excuses not to be here, which is a miss, because every get-together is more than an event or meeting. This is where you dive into the pool of game-changers. You are leaving behind the person you thought you were and becoming the future you. Showing up is now a part of your job description. Step into those shoes and walk into a room and onto the field. The people from your past, the ones who took your shine, are not here. This takes bravery. Plus, you look really good today. Appreciate yourself for doing this for yourself today and for the hard work it took for you to get here.

Stand tall, take a deep breath, and walk in with all your experience. Look around the room and pinpoint the first person you want to meet. If you see a friend, you can start there as a warm-up, but don't spend all of your time with them unless you can recruit that person to help you meet someone new. Sometimes a networking buddy can make the experience easier because you will be tag-teaming.[58]

Game-changers show up over and over again.

Forget about bad past experiences; each meeting, event, and networking experience is entirely new. Did you embarrass yourself in the past? Own it. Treat it lightly and maybe make someone laugh about it.

Keep your agenda simple. Try to accomplish at least one thing from this list, and your time will be well spent.

- *You are here to make a difference for just one person.*
- *You are here to make one great connection.*
- *You are here to learn one great thing.*
- *You are here to meet your next customer or cheerleader.*[59]

OWN YOUR VOICE

You have experience and have done things. It may not be a big thing yet, but you have done some great things and must

---

[58] *This term comes from professional wrestling. A team of two wrestlers who compete one at a time against either member of another such team. So rather than meeting people on your own, you are bringing the party along to people you do not know.*

[59] *In sports, it is a member of a team that performs organized cheering or chanting in support of a sports team. In business, this is the person that speaks well of you in your absence and recommends you to other people.*

proudly wear those accomplishments. People need to hear your story and know of your experience. Your experience could be the one thing that changes a person's life today, and it can also be a wonderful way to make that connection.

Many people have similar stories, and it all works when you find that connection. But you have to speak up and tell your story. Storytelling is one of the most powerful ways to communicate because people remember stories. Storytelling started when people gathered around fires before electricity, and it is used over and over in communication to build friendships today.

Get started by offering someone a compliment. People rarely do this, so you will stand out by making their day. Compliments are incredibly powerful; think about the last time you received one.

Next, do not hide your talent when you are in full swing[60] in a conversation. Speak confidently because you have earned the right to be there. You are a CEO speaking to another CEO, and you have more in common than you think. People get really hung up on trying to get people to like them. Just be yourself; it is the easiest role to play. But if you bring value to every conversation and speak to people as a friend, you will be liked, and you will be memorable.

Think to yourself continuously, "I am here to be delightful. I am a delightful person," because people do not want to be around awful people; it is that easy. Be a little bit of sunshine in their day. Being a ray of sunshine should not

---

[60] *In sports like golf, a "full swing" refers to the complete, full-motion swing used to hit the ball, involving a full rotation of the body and a controlled transfer of energy to the clubhead. Something big could be happening, baby!*

be seen as being weak; that only the super-serious, grouchy people are the ones who succeed. It is not true.

What is true is that you can be absolutely fierce and, at the same time, delightful. There are cases where you will not find your new, next best friend at an event, which is entirely okay because there are millions of people on this planet in business. And in reality, it is not about volume when it comes to connections. It is a few solid connections that get you to the next level. And then a few more. And the people you meet know others who need to know you. So connect with as many people as you can. Assess a room like this:

- *"Okay, this person is great. We have met five times, and we have a relationship. I need to ask them how their vacation went."*
- *"Those two people I don't know at all, so I am going to go over and introduce myself."*
- *"I have met those two once or twice, so I am going to reintroduce myself and check in with them."*
- *"Okay, right now, I can't remember the names of those people, so hopefully, when I reintroduce myself, they will reintroduce themselves too."*

All this connecting can only happen when your voice comes out of your mouth. It is that easy. Work the room, be delightful, be interesting, and be interested. Fun story: I have been told by a new connection, "You are a little upbeat for this time of morning." Meaning, maybe I was a little too much for that person's personality. My response was, "I am! Because I find the alternative to be such a drag." I got a small laugh as he didn't think I would respond like that. We got along great after that.

ACT WITH COURAGE

People always say to work outside of your comfort zone and be brave. So, even if it scares you, do it anyway. Internally, we are all a mess and full of fear, so don't think you are alone in this. Typically, our internal voices send us warnings that are not based on fact. We can absolutely do this.

The ones who get the farthest are the ones who get comfortable with that uncomfortable feeling. It doesn't go away; we simply practice changing the bats flying around in our stomachs into butterflies and accept big and small challenges, knowing that everyone else is trying to do their best too. We are all awkward and afraid of judgment, but we step forward anyway, over and over again, and finally, it becomes natural. We did it, it's over, and we will do it again.

I sometimes think, "What is the worst that could happen?" The answer is typically, "I will embarrass myself." But the odds are that you won't. And if you end up doing something embarrassing, simply own it and take all the power away from the situation. People might laugh if it were genuinely funny, but guess what? You are officially memorable! People's opinion of you in the aftermath is what matters; how you handled an embarrassing situation is how you will truly be remembered. Control the narrative, and take control back quickly. Plus, this will make for a great story later.

Is there a superstar in the room that you want to meet? Get on the starting line[61] and count, "ready, set, go," and work your way close enough to that person for an introduction, and try:

- *"I wanted to come over and congratulate you on ..."*
- *"What you are doing in the community is fantastic. Thank you."*
- *"I have been a huge fan of yours for a while."*
- *"I don't want to take up much of your time; I have always wanted to meet you."*

This may start a conversation with that person, or that may be all you say. Your kindness will be remembered, and it will make their day because people remember kind people. Remember, they think less about what you say and more about how you make them feel.

Speak up. Have the courage to be on a panel or speak in front of a group. When men are asked to speak on panels and in front of groups, they say "yes," but when women are asked, they usually say "no."

Digging into this, women often feel like they are not qualified to speak, and on the other hand, men will tend to ask what the topic is after they have said "yes." Change your game. You are an intelligent person and can offer thoughts on a lot of topics. Say "yes"! The event organizers work hard to get qualified people to speak to their groups, and you have been chosen by reputation or referral.

Panel discussions are easy because if you get stuck, you can toss the question to another panelist because it is their

---

[61] *"Starting line" refers to the line marking the beginning of a race or game. Get those fabulous shoes up there and get ready.*

specialty. You can quickly offer to "take" a question if you know the answer too. I repeat, if asked, say "yes"!

The women in the business community need to see other women on stage. Otherwise, it looks like men have all the answers, and the women just need to listen and learn. Your presence shows other women they can do it too. Most of all, if you were asked to be on stage, then you are the expert they want to hear from.

Can't make it due to a conflict? Be a team player and suggest a substitution, or perhaps give another woman the opportunity to take your place.

Say "yes"! Everyone gets nervous, questions their knowledge, and is too busy to commit. However, the ones that get ahead are the ones that do it anyway.

HUDDLE If you need an extra push of courage, then I highly recommend that you watch the video by Glennon Doyle about "remembering that you are a goddamn cheetah." Better yet, read her book, *Untamed*. You will see your true self in this particular story and be able to approach things with the bravery that you were born with because, when it comes to being the leader you were born to be, you are indeed a "goddamn cheetah."

LEAVE WITH LASTING CONNECTIONS

If you approach every room knowing that we are all human and desire to connect with other humans, the process becomes easy. Dr. Mark A. Williams' book *The Connected Species* is a deep dive into how important it is for all of us to be connected in person with our fellow humans.

This book speaks directly to how we are all a bit damaged from being quarantined from each other, either by the pandemic or relying only on virtual conversations. We have all seen the video of soldiers returning to their families. I am 100 percent sure that up until that point, our warriors either wrote letters or were on video calls with loved ones, but it isn't until they are in the same room with their people that the real connection happens.

Meet people in person, make eye contact, shake hands, and find out what you have in common. Ask questions with easy responses, such as:

- *"What brought you here today?"*
- *"What is it that you do?"*
- *"How long have you been doing this?"*
- *"How did you get to this stage in your career?"*

> **Players greet each other by shaking hands. Do not wait for someone else to do it first.**

This line of questioning can lead you to a path where you find out that you live in the same town, know the same people, went to the same school, or something even more interesting. The key is that people can ease into any conversation with easy answers, and the questions about themselves are the easiest. Don't initially offer up a question that involves a deep answer or sounds like it should be written as a blog.

Another tactic is to be your best detective, figure out the one thing another person is interested in, and base it on the event.

If you are at a golf fundraiser:

- *"Do you play golf?"*
- *"Why do you like it?"*
- *"Where is your favorite place to play?"*

It may eventually get to the point where they ask you if you like to golf. If you do, great! If not, you get to respond with something like, "No. But it is such a popular sport, and I am always curious about the people who play it," or "I've always thought about learning how, but today I am here just to support the cause." Be interested and interesting, and you will make great connections.

WHISTLE! Asking light and different questions sets you apart from everyone else asking, "So, how is business?" If you are this person, you are boring. Yes, I said it. Have fun with the conversation and push it until you can see the limit of where you can go with it.

The don'ts:

- *Don't come on too strong with someone you barely know. Get in there and talk, but read the person or the group and see if you are being too much at this exact time. Think of it like a gentle knead. You can't come in punching.*

- *Don't go from asking questions to a complete interrogation. If you have asked three good questions and the conversation is still a bit weak, thank them for their time and gracefully leave the conversation.*
- *Don't ask, "Do you know what I think?" If you do it too soon, before someone knows you, they won't care what you think. I said what I said. Timing is everything, so let us get to know you a little to see if your opinion is a great add. You can preface a little bit of your background if what you are about to say is an educated contribution.*
- *Don't bring up religion or politics in a business environment. Just don't. The topics of conversation are endless. Avoid these two.*

THE GAME PLAN FOR MEETINGS AND EVENTS

Now is the time to show people what you are made of. You are ready to be noticed. How do you do that? Here is the game plan[62] for meetings:

Tips for meetings:
- *Be happy to be there. Get there early to grab your drink of choice and network; come prepared.*
- *Find your seat immediately to put your things down and move about free of clutter. Of course, pick a seat that has an impact by sitting near the person running the meeting, so they know you are there. Pick a place where you can see and hear everything clearly, and where you will be seen and heard clearly. Stop running for the back row to hide or save the other seats for more important people. If people are milling around and still networking, do the same.*

---

[62] *A strategy worked out in advance. "Winging it" is not a strategy until it all comes completely naturally to you, and it will.*

- *Be in your seat when the meeting starts.*
- *Pay attention and stay engaged.*
- *Don't hide in your phone or your notes.*
- *Listen carefully before contributing, but do contribute.* Not sure where to jump in? Ask clarifying questions. "Just so I understand you ..." People like to know they are being heard, so this should work in your favor to gain respect as a team player. You will be noticed, recognized as paying attention, and interested in the outcome. Go, team!
- *If you can't ask questions immediately, write them down during the meeting so you can ask them later.*
- *Someone might interrupt you while you are talking.* Let's call it an interception.[63] Why? Because business is sports, and having the ball is the main objective. Whoever has the ball is the person people pay attention to, which is why people scramble for it. Having "the ball" means they could score for the team, which can sometimes get rough out there. Remember that this is how the game of business is played. Get the ball back. What you wanted to say was equally important as any ball stealer.
- *If someone steals your idea, get it back.*
  - *"Yes, that is what I was trying to say earlier."*
  - *"That's what I said earlier, so thanks for bringing it back."*
  - *"Thanks for building on my idea."*

  This is the game. Winners and losers. Play as they play. The person with the ball gets the point. Watch a few minutes of almost any sport and see how aggressively players will steal[64] the ball from each other. They also

---

[63] It occurs in American football when the ball gets taken from you while you are in motion, like when that pass lands in the hands of your opponent. Ugh.

[64] Taking the ball away from your opponent. Because you can.

use that same energy to steal it back. Be selective in what you choose to fight for. Sometimes, giving someone an assist[65] is perfectly fine, as business is a team sport. Sometimes it is okay just to let it go and play hard the next time.

People pay attention to people who are paying attention.

Tips for events:

- *Walk in like you are supposed to be there.* Heck, people were waiting for you to get there!

- *Take an immediate attitude of "How can I contribute?"* or "Who in this room can I help?" You have value, and someone in that room will need to hear from you. Don't just show up to check the box of being there.

- *Talk to people.* Forget your phone, shake someone's hand, and say "hi" to someone. Be aware that in some cultures and in old etiquette books, a man will not extend his hand to shake a woman's hand first. The #metoo movement also made men take a step back from unwanted contact. Break the wall and extend your hand first; show you are here to play, making it a real handshake, because this is how we greet each other in business sports ball. "Hi, I'm Catherine, and it is great to meet you."

- *Afraid of making a mistake or doing something foolish?* Own it. Immediately. Be comfortable with your imperfection because people will like you more if you own it. You are taking the pressure off of everyone who needs to be perfect. Having said, "That was a

---

[65] An assist is a pass or setup play that helps a teammate score a point in a sport. Assists are a key statistic that show teamwork and a player's contribution to the team's scoring. While another person is getting the point, this works in your favor on so many levels. I'm talking to you as a team player, cheerleader, champion, or overall great human.

terrible handshake; can I try that again?" put everyone immediately at ease. Or "Darn it, Tom, I called you Jay! And I knew your name. I don't know where my head is lately."

- **Are you still feeling like a wallflower?** Find another wallflower and talk with them to get warmed up. Work the room together as a team. "Hi, I am Catherine. Did you come here by yourself?" Add some small talk. "Let's finish this drink and go meet some people together." The bar, the buffet table, and the coffee station are all great places to start a conversation with people you don't know.

- **Be happy to see people.** "Resting bitch face" is a real thing, and I have a great one. Do you have one? Think happy thoughts to combat it. Do you know how excited your dog or cat is to see you when you get home? Think about that kind of happiness. Everyone wants to be seen and appreciated, and you will be memorable if you are pleasant and friendly.
  - "Hey, I've heard of you."
  - "I've heard of your company."
  - "I've been wanting to meet you."
  - "I am so excited to meet you."

- **Be interested and interesting.** People love to talk about themselves, so ask questions and be interested in their responses. If you keep it that simple, it takes a lot of pressure off you regarding conversations and conversation starters.
  - "How are you doing today?"
  - "Have you been to one of these events before?"
  - "What is your business?"
  - "That is interesting. What do you do there?"

- *"How did you get into this career?"*
- *Be curious and genuine; at some point, you should be able to see where you can help them with a connection or simply find a new ally. They might have a connection for you, or maybe they will be that future customer.*
- *Sit up front. It doesn't have to be in the front row, but choose a seat where not only the speaker can see you but everyone in the room can too. Yikes! I know, but you do want to be seen, and seen, and seen. When you are seen often, people come to you with conversations and opportunities. When you are pleasant, people will want to be around you. When you are wearing that power outfit you picked out earlier, that one that practically makes you an emoji of yourself, you will be recognized. Be seen everywhere, and then people will see you as a game-changer.*
- *Travel light. Keep everything in pockets or a light handbag. At networking events, people will try to juggle a drink, a plate, a purse, a notebook, a coat, etc. Work toward having one hand free to shake hands at all times. On the other hand, having a drink of any kind, even water, is a simple way of telling the crowd that you are here to participate. Are you a fan of a giant purse? Leave it at home and take the bare minimum of what you need. You are not the equipment manager.*[66]

Nervousness about events is typically based on past experiences or fear of not being liked. Think less about whether people will like you and more about whether or not you will like them. Have the mindset that you are there to connect and help others. The best teams are built on mutual respect.

---

[66] *An equipment manager is responsible for overseeing all equipment used by a business or organization; they also handle uniforms, gear, and ensure athletes are properly fitted.*

HUDDLE

How do you want to be seen in meetings and at events? Here are some things to try that worked for me:

- *Posture.* Amy Cuddy wrote a book, *Presence*, about the importance of being present and owning your space. Don't be small, and don't sit like you are disinterested. Again, people pay attention to people who pay attention. Amy's book gives the reader an exercise to stand in a "Wonder Woman pose" before you need to do a big thing. Science may debate the effectiveness of this, but it worked for me. Need to make a big speech? Walk around like Wonder Woman for about ten minutes right before your challenge. Have a tough conversation coming up? Stand in the bathroom in that hands-on-hips pose for a bit while walking around. You can also stretch your arms and legs to make yourself as big as possible. The pose changes your thinking, posture, and attitude, and that exercise alone can propel you to take on something you might not have been able to.

- *Dress the part.* People in the big leagues[67] look put together, like they belong in the room of decision-makers. Dressing the part is not all about an expensive wardrobe but about clean, tasteful, and well-fitting clothes. It is simple. Let them see the real you and not the latest fashion trend. If you are unsure about what style to go with,

---

[67] *The top tier of play, typically at a professional level.*

think about who you admire or find an image of a woman in leadership that fits your style, the style of how you want to be perceived. Take off the look of the present day you and emulate the person you want to be, the future you. We can only become who we want to be if we let go of who we currently are. After 5:00 p.m., those fuzzy slippers and sweatpants can go right back on, I insist. This thinking falls in line with the saying, "Dress for the job that you want." You will be dressing to match the vibe of the decision-makers, the game-changers, and the big thinkers. I mean, you have already earned it; just accept the promotion. If money is an issue for clothes, you don't have to go crazy. Look for sales, look into consignment shops, places that have donated business clothing, or a friend's closet, but it needs to be one outfit that makes you look and feel like a player. You can also invest in a few key pieces. My look was simple: tailored black clothes, bold lipstick, and statement eyeglasses, and I did it every single time. It might seem boring, and it might have been the same few pieces that I rotated, but creating an emoji of yourself only makes you more memorable. Basically, I made myself memorable by always looking the same, making it very easy for me to be recognized. If you are still struggling with a look, contact your favorite store and ask if they can help you put together an outfit you feel good in. I cannot tell you how much the store employees will love that you asked. More on clothes later.

- *Language.* Speak at a general audience level until you know your audience, or don't speak "over their heads" because you want to sound like an expert. They won't hear a thing. Talk slower than usual, and take your time to choose the right words. We tend to speak fast when we are nervous; for some of us, we tend to speak fast all of the time. Be intentional with your words, and don't be afraid of pausing. Be aware of when it is time to speak like a professional and when it is time to make it more casual. Which makes this a good time to talk about swearing. I love a good swear word. Sometimes, it is the perfect word for the occasion. Swear words can be distracting, and you have one chance to make that first impression; you only want them to hear what you can contribute without distraction. A swear word can hang in the air longer than the event itself, so as challenging as it might be under certain circumstances, hold those spicy words in.

- *Speak with real involvement.* When it is your turn to speak, speak from the diaphragm and not in a whisper. Speak confidently, clearly, and directly. Make eye contact. Get to the point, and don't go on a tangent, because you will lose your audience. Don't be afraid to jump into a conversation if you have something valuable to add, and don't wait too long to speak up because you are taking too long to evaluate whether you have something of value to add. You are in a conversation, not giving a presentation. Ask other people's opinions if you see someone in the group who has not spoken up. People remember the people who include others.

- *Know when to move on.* Time is limited at events, and the room is full of potential new friends. Spend five or ten minutes talking to someone, and if there is more to be said, longer is okay. Be prepared to exchange information and plan on getting together at a later date. Be the social butterfly, jump from flower to flower, and linger when you have a great conversation. Get good at excusing yourself because sometimes you need to move on quickly.
  - *"I don't want to take up any more of your time, but thank you, I loved our conversation."*
  - *"It has been great talking to you, but there is someone here that I must speak to."*

Again, avoid all conversations about politics or religion, just like our moms told us to do. And regardless of who the person is, if it gets creepy, leave the conversation quickly.

Showing up and participating only works when we don't deny[68] ourselves success or commit self-sabotage. Be mindful that sometimes our desire to be liked can push us

---

[68] *In basketball it is actively stopping a pass to an opponent.*

into people-pleasing mode. We start giving away all our time helping and volunteering. The results only elevate the other person; you need to be here for you.

If you keep telling people "yes" to what they want you to do, what are you saying "no" to in your own life? Every meeting and every event should not be only a drain on your time. If you are out among people, you shake hands, find champions, and help them out. Make sure that you are getting something out of it too. Helping others is an amazing gift. We all need to do this, but not at the expense of ourselves.

We tend to overwork to prove our value and feel like we are enough, but if you look around and are the only one who stays late and delivers, you may need to rethink the relationship with those around you. Live your own story; don't follow someone else's script. You are the star, not the sidekick. "Can I get back to you on that?" is an absolutely valid way to buy more time for yourself to see if you can commit to something.

WHISTLE! Give people the impression that you are just stopping by for a "hello" and that you are very busy. This gives you the opportunity to choose whether to stay or move on.

There is a difference between participating and playing to win; other people can tell the difference. And if you are not brave enough to say that you want to win, it may be a matter of not knowing your purpose. The next step in your growth would be figuring out your purpose and your "why."

Simon Sinek wrote a book called *Find Your Why?* Order it, get it from the library, or watch his video today if you don't know why you are doing what you are doing in your career or business. Not knowing your purpose could be the one thing that is keeping you stuck, because if you are doing something that really lights you up, you become truly driven to make things happen.

Knowing your "why" or your purpose is also the best way to determine if you are on the right path. You want to show up for yourself and those around you with your purpose. If you are hungry to do more, learn more, and challenge yourself to be better, you will keep improving. What happens next is magical because the people around you see your passion and possibly share your purpose, and they need a leader to show them the way. Without asking permission, you put yourself in the pole position,[69] and when you are in the front, you get noticed. Then, once you know your "why," things fall into place quickly.

Now, what if your purpose does not align with your business? You can think about working with charities that align with your passion as a board member, committee member, or volunteer. You can choose to donate to your favorite charity in your client's name as a holiday gift. Applying your purpose and your superpowers to this kind of service will also elevate you in the eyes of the community, and it doesn't take much. You can dedicate some of your time to building awareness for an organization if marketing is your strength. This is also another new group of people that you can get to know to build your business or career.

---

[69] *The very coveted, very front spot in a race, typically in motorsports where you are in the front and on the inside of the track, giving you an edge over your competitors.*

Once you know why you are here on the planet, figuring out where you fit is simple problem-solving. Do you believe in supporting women? You could hire some stay-at-home moms because they are professionals looking to contribute. Do you have a passion for animals? You can plan a team outing to an animal shelter. Maybe you can have your team bring their pet to work. Do you feel strongly about your alma mater? You could have summer internships for students in need of experience. Connect the dots.

Regardless of your passion, you must participate in meetings and networking events that keep up your momentum and get you seen by others. That is simply how it works and the way I approached it. If you are asked to be in the room or paid to be in the room, make it a good use of your time. Otherwise, why be there? You can try to incorporate your "why" in these meetings. Or it could be something that will wait until later.

RULE #3: YOUR PROFESSIONAL UNIFORM MAKES YOU RECOGNIZABLE

Somewhere behind the athlete you've become and the hours of practice and the coaches who have pushed you is the little girl who fell in love with the game and never looked back. ... Play for her.

—Mia Hamm, two-time Olympic gold medalist and two-time FIFA Women's World Cup champion

Y ou are showing up and making connections; now, you need to consider your uniform, your way of being identified, or your personal brand. A personal brand is the intentional and consistent way an individual presents themselves to the world, encompassing their skills, values, experiences, and the overall impression they aim to create, influencing how others perceive and remember them.

In consumer goods, having a brand is crucial. Band-Aid, Nike, and Spanx are all strong brands that immediately create an image in your head when someone says their name. You need that kind of recognition, in how you look and how people feel about you too. You are recognized in meetings and events for your professional look. Still, you also want people to recognize you as an expert, as a kind, intelligent, driven, and exciting person they want to hang around with.

You always look put together. You may have a trademark look, such as big glasses, Converse shoes, or you are always seen in Gucci. You consciously err toward being slightly overdressed or as one of the best-dressed in the room. You connect with people because you are pleasant and upbeat.

This is your brand, what people expect from you when they see you, and what people say about you when you are not in the room. This is how you show up every time, regardless of the day you are having. This is the time for your game face[70] because the best leaders are the ones who appear unflappable.

As pure children, before the world taught us about negativity, we were invincible. Somewhere along the way, we were told to:

- *Sit and be quiet.*
- *Be polite.*
- *Play nice.*
- *Act like a lady.*

---

[70] *The expression that you put on when you are going to try to win or achieve something.*

- *That's not for girls.*
- *Boys will be boys.*
- *Know your place.*
- *Your main job is as a wife and mother.*
- *Be the caregiver.*
- *Be the nurturer.*

And for the knock-out:[71]

- *You are not worthy.*
- *You are not smart enough.*
- *Do you think that you are better than me?*
- *You and your crazy ideas.*
- *You don't have what it takes.*
- *Men are better leaders.*

But guess what? Everyone who spoke to you like that thought they controlled your story, and from now on, you are in charge of your story. Personal branding differs from regular branding in that it is your story that takes center stage, and it is your history that is interesting, even when you don't think it is. Your story and every moment before this very moment can be mentioned as part of your brand and storytelling experience.

Everyone loves a story when someone can overcome a huge hurdle.[72] Think about it: How terrible would a book be if the protagonist didn't overcome anything or face any challenges? Boring. So forget about the pitfalls you have experienced, as they no longer hold you back, but instead,

---

[71] *A term used in boxing where a fighter is hit so hard they get knocked out, fall to the mat, and the fight is over.*

[72] *In track and field a hurdle is those fence-like things that people can jump over while running. Comfortable shoes are recommended.*

this is what has prepared you for this exact moment of your life. We all have our own great story, and when it matches up to other people's great stories, we have made a great connection.

> There were times when I had to put everything on the line to get what I wanted, sometimes starting from complete scratch. But I had enough faith in my ability to know that I could take the leap to get closer to my dream.

My story is mainly about always looking higher. Even when I was content or, in most cases, still wanted more, I kept trying to figure out a way to get to where I needed and wanted to go. I had to start from broke a few times. All those struggles and attempts to break free are part of my story. Everything that got me here may not have happened if I changed one good or one lousy thing.

> Sometimes the things you deal with are horrible, but you must walk through that fire to get where you need to go.

For me, moving up involved making big moves and taking baby steps. It meant working really hard when I could have been doing more fun things, getting out of a marriage that was destroying me, getting married again to a person who actually supported me, and raising a child while figuring out how to start and grow a business and get all of the laurels that go along with that. One thing led to another, leading to another. It is a twisted, challenging, crazy story that is all mine, and your story is all yours.

WHY NOT YOU?

Think about a brand that you use or feel strongly about. It probably has a story about an entrepreneur who started with an idea and set up shop in their garage. Some of these entrepreneurs had immediate backing, and some bootstrapped their ideas, but all have a story about their passion, fear, growth, and how they wanted to be perceived in the world. They are all great origin stories, with a great story arc that leads to success.

> **Failure occurs when you quit, not when you try.**

HUDDLE Your story might be simple or a real page-turner. Where to start? We start with the young girl that you were. If you need to, find photos of yourself to really remember who you were before everyone tried to write your story. Sometimes, those photos are helpful to see when someone else tried to write your story, so you can identify what exactly happened, how fear began, or who the person was who made a positive difference in your life. If you don't have photos, find photos online of games you used to play: Twister, tag, Clue, jump rope, Barbie, Legos, anything that will trigger these youthful memories.

Work on answering these questions. Give yourself time to respond. This exercise builds an awareness of the inner you as a starting point.

1. How would you describe your personality at age five?
2. How would you describe your personality at age sixteen?
3. How would you describe your personality now?
4. If money were no object, how would you dress every day?
5. If there were no rules, how would you wear your hair?
6. How would people describe your personality?
7. How do people react when you walk into the room?
8. How would you want people to react when you walked into the room?
9. What is your biggest fear about entering a room of people you don't know?
10. What would that younger version of you think about you now, at this age? Is she proud, sad, impressed, etc?

These answers are the pieces of ourselves that we sometimes lose and can be the foundation for building our personal brand. These things are the foundation of our origin story. We want to recapture this pure energy, the dreams we had for ourselves before people or society tried to shape us, and start incorporating these things back into our daily lives because these are the things that make us uniquely us. It is that uniqueness that is going to make you stand out. It is the unique people who made history.

How we talk, dress, and the energy we bring when entering a room are all a part of our story. That story may be the one someone else wrote for us or the one we are writing for ourselves, but wherever it came from, it is how we got here and has worked to get us this far. Now we need to dig in to get us to the next level, start writing our next chapter, and grab the spirit of that little girl we left behind long ago.

The questions above will help us assess how comfortable we are entering a room and the expectations of ourselves and others. We could enter as the wallflower, the shot of whiskey, the dignitary, the loud mouth; we could enter as fearful or as a force. What is most important is that we run onto the field[73] with enthusiasm and as our unique selves so people can form an impression about who we are and what we are made of. That impression is formed in a fraction of a second, which is why our personal brand is so important.

The belief system that we have about ourselves runs deep and needs to be dissected in order to make significant changes. Over forty years ago, family therapist and author Richard C. Schwartz wrote *No Bad Parts*. He came up with the idea of IFS, or Internal Family Systems. Schwartz believes that we all have multiple perspectives within us. He uses the example of people often identifying with their inner critic, worrier, or striver. He teaches that we must embrace all parts of ourselves rather than letting one of those "voices" dominate our lives.

---

[73] *The designated area of land marked out for playing a particular game, essentially the playing surface where the action of the sport takes place, often including boundaries and markings specific to the game. Sometimes called a "pitch" depending on the sport. If you think a man can be touchy about his lawn, just stay off the field or pitch.*

This theory played out once again in a book written by Jill Bolte Taylor, Ph.D., called *Whole Brain Living*. In the book, she tells the story of how having a stroke resulted in her, as a doctor, being able to physically experience only the duties that align with the right side of her brain, as the left side of her brain was temporarily dormant.

The book overall is about her experience and her knowledge of brain function because, as a doctor, she had a perspective like no one else. She learned from herself as she temporarily operated with only the creative, risk-taking, carefree side of her brain. What I love most about this book is the exercise she offers in understanding our own brains that starts with seeing the brain being divided into four quadrants, each giving us messages in the form of different "personalities." The brain is vastly complex, so this really distills everything down for better understanding.

In her book, she has an exercise for identifying your personalities to get your whole brain working together. I have distilled it down to make this exercise, but to go deeper with this and more, I definitely recommend the book.

HUDDLE As you read the words listed below, think whether a character or person you know comes to mind. We will then find images of people that match these words, so be prepared to find photos of each character or player[74] online or in your own personal photo collection so you can bring them to life. These characters do things to influence you, protect you, and inspire you.

---

[74] *A player in a sport or game is a person who takes part. Each member has a specific function that they excel at. People that cannot play do not last very long on the team.*

Most people are familiar with the simple breakdown of the brain by saying that the left side is where science, tech, engineering, and math reside. The right side is for creativity, fun, adventure, and joy. This exercise breaks those two halves into two more pieces, totaling four personalities or "voices" in our brain. Let's start with the left.

The left side contains two characters, a thinking character and an emotional character, and these are some of the characteristics that are attached to each one:

Left Thinking Character #1

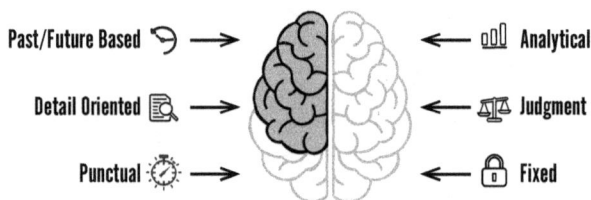

Past/Future Based →	← Analytical
Detail Oriented →	← Judgment
Punctual →	← Fixed

Left Emotional Character #2

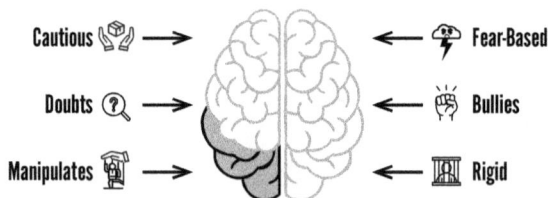

Cautious →	← Fear-Based
Doubts →	← Bullies
Manipulates →	← Rigid

The right side also contains two characters, a thinking character and an emotional character, and these are the characteristics that are assigned to this side:

Right Thinking Character #1

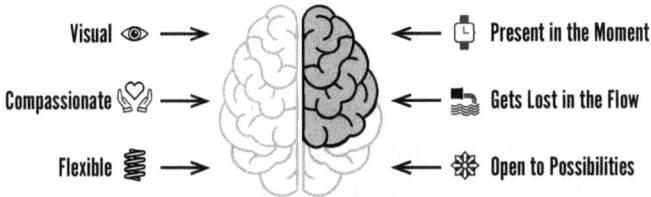

Visual ◉ →   ← ⌚ Present in the Moment

Compassionate 🤲 →   ← 🌊 Gets Lost in the Flow

Flexible 🧬 →   ← ❄️ Open to Possibilities

Right Emotional Character #2

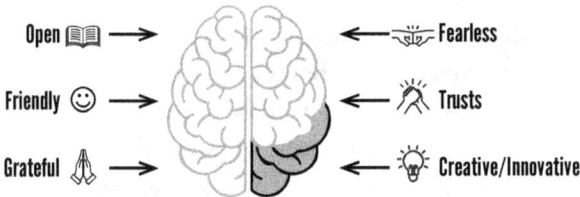

Open 📖 →   ← ⚖️ Fearless

Friendly ☺ →   ← 🏹 Trusts

Grateful 🙏 →   ← 💡 Creative/Innovative

Do any people or characters come to mind when you read the words associated with each quadrant?

- *Left Thinking Character:* This one is like a worker, the warrior within us, the one who likes to always be the front runner,[75] the "get it done" person and the one who is driven.
- *Left Emotional Character:* This personality doubts our capabilities, keeps us fearful of growing bigger, and manipulates or bullies[76] us. This character holds on to our impostor syndrome. It also tries to protect us from hurting ourselves, like "I don't think that you can make that jump," to "I wouldn't try that if I were you."
- *Right Thinking Character:* This personality loves what they do and is willing to try anything. They are the cheerleaders [77] in your life.
- *Right Emotional Character:* This warm and welcoming character isn't afraid of anything and can even be endless when coming up with ideas. They are the problem-solvers and the playmakers[78] because their creativity can become strategies to win.

---

[75] *Refers to the leader in a race or competition.*

[76] *Bullying in sports takes all forms and has been commonplace for decades. It can be physical, verbal, or emotional.*

[77] *The cheerleader is there to motivate sports teams, to entertain the audience, or for competition. They are balls of energy.*

[78] *The playmakers have the ability to read the game, improvise plays, and set up scoring opportunities for teammates, requiring a high level of vision and decision-making under pressure. So necessary and so you.*

I will go through this exercise with my results to help you better visualize it. When reading those words and hearing those descriptions, my characters came very easily to me. I read the characteristics, and the face appeared.

At my brain's conference table, I have:

- *My Left-Thinking Character #1* is *Brienne of Tarth*, a character in the *Game of Thrones* who is completely loyal and relentless. She is the driven part of me, the fighter. She was the loudest voice in my head for most of my career, knowing the mission and not stopping until it was finished. Always pushing forward and not living in the now, she will fight, push, drive, and repeat because she will not rest until all of the work is done. Her analytical strength keeps her strategizing and looking for ways to get ahead.

- *My Left Emotional Character #2* is *Sue Sylvester* from the television show *Glee*. Sue is a coach who will never let you forget you are not trying hard enough, you probably aren't good enough, and don't even know why you even try. She will remind me of how I failed to do something in the past and warn me about pitfalls I could encounter. She is also a bit of a protector; she will fight me so I am afraid to try new things or keep me from repeating mistakes that I have made in the past to protect me from failure. She holds the keys to my impostor syndrome.

- *My Right Thinking Character #3* is whimsical, fun, friendly, and adventurous. In my head, she is best compared to *Phoebe Buffay* from the television show *Friends*. Phoebe is the keeper of our passions. She is always present in the moment and open to possibilities. She is clever, creative, and funny. All her feelings are front and center, and it is very easy for her to get lost in the flow when working on a passion project. She enjoys the moment that she is in.

- *My Right Emotional Character #4* is the fearless one, a creative genius in seeing opportunities, and our most trusting character. My icon for this character is one we all know as the singer *Dolly Parton*. The Dolly Parton in my head is similar to the one we all see: giving, empathetic, and creating ways to help others, while being a shrewd businesswoman. She is wildly creative and the ultimate problem-solver. She is fearless when doing what she feels is right and builds friendships and connections along the way. She is incredibly grateful and giving to others.

I need all of these characters to succeed in business and to have a healthy life, but getting all of them to talk equally can be a challenge when I operate from a place of comfort with one of those voices. Let's join *Brienne, Sue, Phoebe, and Dolly* sitting at a small conference table.

My Brienne runs the meetings and has controlled the conversation and most of my actions all my life. She knows that if we just work harder and put in more hours, we can get exactly what we want, which means I struggle with being in the moment, taking the time to be creative, and growing in other ways because I am too busy being busy. Take a vacation? Don't be ridiculous; there is too much to do.

By doing this exercise, all I saw was Brienne talking. I could then see that most of my time was spent having my nose to the grindstone. Greatness doesn't come from the strongest characters constantly trying to hog the ball[79] and trying to do all of the scoring. That character will be running the same play repeatedly with the exact same results. Instead, if we collaborate with everyone in our heads, we can outsmart competitors, create new strategies, and move mountains. Everything we want to accomplish should be run past the team so we can vet it for strength, poke holes in the idea, and get excited about the possibilities. Every part of our brain needs to be utilized for the desired results; otherwise, we are working too hard.

Here is a simple example of how they all talk together:

- *Left front: Let's go, let's get started.*
- *Left back: I have identified some concerns.*
- *Right front: This is a crazy idea, and I love it; let me know what you need from me.*
- *Right back: I have an idea about this, and the potential is going to be great.*

---

[79] *Hogging the ball is a term used in team sports to describe a player who keeps the ball to themselves instead of passing it to their teammates. Ball hogs may dribble the ball excessively and take difficult shots, especially when other players are in better positions. Ew. No one wants to be a "hog" of anything.*

Many women get stuck when the *Sue Sylvester* character walks in with doubt and impostor syndrome. This character is vital because she holds on to all the lessons learned and warns us about repeating ourselves; for example, how we are always attracted to that guy or gal that breaks our hearts, but we keep falling for them. She is in control of "gut feelings" and instinct, and is excellent at what she does. But we need to make sure that she is not running the entire meeting and keeping us from stepping out of our comfort zone.

"Don't do that. Remember what happened last time?" If it is about touching a stove, it is a good thing. If it is about trying to stretch your wings or climb higher, you need to get your group back together and figure out how you will do it. Create a plan, take an adventure, have fun trying, find joy in seeing what could happen, and make sure that all of your characters are contributing. Women talk all the time about being ignored in meetings, and this is the opportunity for you to include everyone in your meetings.

Now let's identify your team. My people are my people, so select other representations that will resonate with you. This could be characters from your favorite show or movie; it could be one of your old teachers, a family member, or a person you only met once.

Reread the characteristics and find photos to represent those people around your house or on the Internet. These characters know everything about you, every fear and every dream. Find the images, print them, and put them in a place where you can access them quickly. Seeing the physical photos helps us connect more with these chosen characters by visualizing them and feeling what they represent to us.

In our minds, they are all sitting in our brain at a conference table, and in most cases, one of them runs the meeting, and one or two sit silently. This is when we get off balance, and we need to open the conversation to everyone so they can all collaborate to get us where we need to go. We need all of them talking and contributing because each player, coach, and behind-the-scenes worker brings a unique perspective and plays together to achieve the win. Who in your own brain has been the most dominant, and who has been kept silent for so long? With every action, determine how you can have them all contribute.

If you identify some of those characters as people in your own life, think about how they planted seeds of doubt or pushed you higher. See their face when you get caught up in weak thoughts of self-sabotage. Identifying a face to look at starts the process of having a conversation with our own doubts and fears. We all have these thoughts and will self-sabotage when we get uncomfortable. Some of the most powerful reasons I have heard people say to stop their drive forward are:

- *"Remember when I tried something new the last time?"*
- *"I don't think I can do that, it's not me, it feels too bold."*
- *"I'm scared to try."*

- *"I would probably just embarrass myself."*
- *"I don't have time to try new things, I'll stick with what I know works."*

Break this line of thinking and let your other voices speak.
- *"Let's try it. What's the worst thing that can happen?"*
- *"I know if I get pointed in the right direction, I will get it done."*
- *"We are trying something new, and it is exciting."*
- *"We need to do this; we deserve this."*
- *"Do we want it? Then let's figure out how to get it."*

John C. Maxwell was known for saying, *"Teamwork makes the dream work,"* and he could not be more correct. Utilize your entire brain's trust of characters because more of the same is not going to make a change.

Another example: Michael Jordan[80] knew that he was the best player of his time, but when he tried to do it all himself, he lost out on championships. He could not obtain that championship ring until he had his team together with the guidance of Phil Jackson, his coach. Don't let one player "hog the ball" on your team; instead, make passes, set up plays, and score! This is where those voices on the right side of the brain can step up. Those parts of your brain think bigger and know your heart and what your true desires are. Let them speak up! Understanding why you do things and think things is the key to unlocking yourself from certain behaviors.

---

[80] *Michael Jordan, the iconic basketball superstar known for his unmatched athleticism and competitive drive, revolutionized the game while winning six NBA championships. He was also an Olympian and is now a successful businessman.*

One problem you might have is that the workers and the doubters in your head have gotten so strong that the creative, free spirit within you is only a whisper. There is a way to correct that course. I have had the privilege to talk with lots of business leaders and successful entrepreneurs about how they balance hard work with creativity. Rather than working countless hours all of the time, they make space for their own right-brained activities of choice. They understand clearly that only using half of their brain means doing twice the work. Think about trying to get up from a chair using only one leg. It is a lot harder than using both of your legs. So use your whole brain.

That means learning to spend time with our right-brained talents, our inner creativity, to ideate, innovate, problem-solve, strategize, and properly rest. If we allow that side to get dormant, we will just keep repeating the same things and hoping for a different outcome. We need to keep our right-brained voices strong in order to ideate, create new pathways, and be excellent at problem-solving.

CHOOSE THE TEAM TO HELP YOU WIN

Now that we have our brain team together, we can examine the people with whom we physically surround ourselves. I have a whole chapter dedicated to surrounding ourselves with cheerleaders and champions, so for now, let's just talk about the doubters.

Some people will never understand your drive. Your choices were ones that people around you were too afraid to make for themselves, so they created doubt in your head. They say things to hold you back like:

- *"I guess we didn't provide a good enough life for you."*
- *"You are too good for us now."*
- *"I saw your new fancy car. I don't know how you can afford that thing."*
- *"You don't have time to keep a house this big clean."*
- *"Easy for you to say with all of your money."*

It is that constant chipping away, letting self-doubt sneak in the cracks, that stops our forward movement. I have no doubt that my mother loved me; she just didn't understand me. It really is no different when you try to lose weight and your friends sabotage your diet. They love you, but they don't want you to leave them.

> **Other people's issues are other people's issues.**

Creating your best life is your number one mission, and if you are one of those self-sacrificing people dedicated to serving others, let me tell you, you cannot do your best job if you are not at your best. If you fear making mistakes, I can confirm that predicting mistakes does not make them happen. Also, mistakes get made by the greats, and the greats become smarter and more experienced and keep rolling. The loving relationships you enter into will have mistakes, but they will grow stronger because you know what you are learning personally, and you can help someone else grow.

Be aware that people in your life may be holding you back, and then be smart about who you need to cut from your team.[81] You need to build a team around you that will help you get better. Family and friends should be there for you, but that doesn't always happen, so you need to make adjustments if they sabotage your success. Remove them from being the main characters in your story because *you* need to be the main character in your story. People who love you will take you higher, not hold you down. They won't pick the flower to admire it; they will give it what it needs to grow and multiply.

> **If they are afraid of your excellence, that is okay because you don't have to be.**

A conversation you can have with your "brain team" beyond "who is holding us back?" is about "what habits should we quit?" What do we say "yes" to that we don't want to do? Saying "yes" to something means you are probably saying "no" to something else. Make room for your own plans in your own story. Once you have all of this sorted, you can bask in the fun of making your story a fairy-tale come true.

One way that women notoriously become minor characters in their own lives is when they say "yes" to others too much. Saying "yes" to help others is an amazing thing. Life is all about working together. But occasionally, we have too much on our plates of our own choice.

Practice saying "no" to a task you don't want to do. Start by asking yourself these questions:

---

[81] *To remove a person from a group or team, usually in a competitive setting like sports, because they are not performing well enough or do not fit the necessary criteria to remain on the roster.*

- *If someone wants your commitment in a month, would you still want to do it if you had to do it today? The idea is that if today is a "no," later is probably a "no" that you are just not facing.*
- *If you say "yes" to this, what are you saying "no" to? Are you giving up time with family, your own work, or some evening plans? Time is valuable and limited; choose wisely. Saying "yes" to things that are an investment in your future is worth it. Just don't overload.*
- *What could you do with the extra time when you say "no" to something? That extra time could be used toward writing a book, attending an event, writing out a nomination for an award, working with a board of your choice, reading a book, or getting back into that hobby you had to sideline because you are always too busy.*

Try spending as much time as possible doing things that make you happy. Really run the numbers[82] on each thing you take on. Life has a way of challenging us, and it will happen without our control. Try to control your time as much as you can.

> **Having life balance is really having life boundaries.**

For all good and fair play, there needs to be boundaries.[83] Studies are available that report how not creating boundaries and always living on the thoughts and actions conducted by

---

[82] *Analyzing and interpreting statistical data to gain insights into player performance, team strategy, or even betting odds. In this case, does it add up to something that you really want to do AND fulfill growth and purpose?*

[83] *In sports, boundaries are the lines that mark the edges of the playing field, as well as the rules and codes of conduct that govern the game.*

the left-brain characters can lead to depression. Think about that. Think about how you feel mentally and physically when you spend eight or more hours working, and then the feeling you have when you unplug that side of your head for the day.

Sometimes, our protective, fear-based character really has its boot on our neck. I have two recommendations that helped me. Read Brené Brown's book *Dare to Lead* or *I Thought It Was Just Me (but It Isn't)*. Brené has over twenty years of experience talking about the unreal quest for perfection and the baggage of shame. It deals with our unrelenting need for perfection, why we doubt ourselves, and more.

Finally, talk to a mental health specialist if you have a trunk full of issues rather than a little baggage. You will be amazed how quickly they can lighten your mental load, and speaking to a specialist no longer has the stigma that it used to. In-person and virtual sessions are more affordable, more accessible, and often covered by insurance. I have gone a few rounds to break bad thinking and bad habits, and it worked.

> **Your brain is like any other organ in your body and needs care too.**

BE READY AND SHOW UP IN YOUR UNIFORM

It sounds unbelievable, but you can shape your personal brand with these tools in place. We might be constructing it from the ground up. We will create your public personality, an alter ego, the one who overcomes the flaws and gains more control. So much of this is based on your past narrative.

As women, we know that in order to play the game, we have to wear the uniform.[84] At the very beginning of my career, all of the women dressed like the men. Fast-forward to owning my own business, and I fully admit that I lost a lot of my personality in the way that I presented myself in my hair, dress, and makeup. I began by wearing what I thought was the uniform of a CEO, and it was a great place to start, but it really was not me. My left brain was my initial fashion consultant, and my look was more about blending in rather than that of my real personality. But when I got four voices involved in the decision process, I was able to make choices that were a better fit for me from a personality standpoint and a little more daring in order to stand out. Create your look in a way that best exhibits your personality.

First impressions are the most difficult, and there is a bit of a strategy involved. The idea is to give them nothing to judge about you other than your personality. For your first time in front of a group, if you normally go bold, dial back your look until you can read the room. Your personality can be and should be your most memorable thing, not your clothes. Another strategy is to mirror others, see how they are showing up, and add a bit of your personality.

In some cases, you don't know what to expect. You walk into the room, and everyone is way more casual than you expected. Adjust accordingly. But honestly, there is nothing wrong with being the best-dressed, most prepared person either. Study the room, see how the rest

---

[84] *Clothing worn by members of the same organization or group.*

of the crowd operates, and then jump into the deep end. Your flexibility and adaptability all come from those right-brained characters. This is all personal brand building with an adjustable game plan.[85]

Look around and determine who is successful in this room and how they are conducting themselves. In sports, the rookies[86] watch the pros to get better. Listen to the type of conversation that is taking place and determine if it is all casual or all business. Tapping into the flow of the room will give you the most traction. Remember that you are working on your public personality, possibly tapping into your alter ego and behaving how the "future you" should be acting right now.

This is how the game is played, and it gets more fun, so hold on.

Once you start to build your image of showing up, paying attention, and being super professional, you can branch out. Based on what you know about your field of interest and the successful people in it, think about how you can deliver something uniquely you. Think about what you want to be known for and what you want to stand for. Think about how you want people to talk about you when you are not in the room.

Evaluate everything you have done up until now and determine what you are good at, what you are an expert in, what your passion is, and what special team[87] you would be

---

[85] A game plan in sports is a strategy that outlines a team's goals, tactics, and roles for a game.

[86] A rookie is typically considered needing more training and learning, though they may bring a new outside expertise to a job.

[87] Special teams are groups of players on a sports team that perform specific plays, such as only kicking or returning the ball.

on. If you are challenged with choosing a specialty, I would recommend taking the "strengths" test at strengthfindertest. com. It will take twenty minutes and provide some strengths worth reflecting on. Having done the test myself, it was pretty accurate, and I used these in my personal messaging for what I wanted to be known for.

The idea of the strengths test is to direct you to work on the things you are really good at rather than trying to get better at things you are not so good at. It basically frees up your time so you can learn to fly faster and higher. There is also a *StrengthsFinder* book to accompany the test and to dig deeper into how you can utilize your strengths.

You are now ready to step up to the plate.[88]

I remember walking into meetings and events with a look that was expected of someone in my position: shift dress, jacket, designer shoes, and hair in a very controlled style. Then, the more I got involved, the more I wanted more of my personality back. You need to meet with your four personalities to determine how you want to walk in the room. Decide on what we are going to own and where we are not going to cross the line. For example, if my four personalities could give one word to describe my outfit, they would be powerful, comfortable, tailored, and a touch of bling.

As described above, "beginner me" was super cute and had designer purses. After a mental meeting, we decided that at the deepest part of my soul, I am an artist, a creative, and a visionary, and I needed to dress like one. I wanted my persona not to be cute but to be a strong businesswoman

---

[88] *To accept a challenge or responsibility for something; to rise to the occasion.*

who, if asked to be on your team, could be the perfect asset for strategy, out-of-the-box thinking, creative solutions, responsible, reliable, and cool-looking enough for people to want to hang around with me. A bona fide uniform and super suit.

My standard blazers and shift dresses were all gone. My clothes were still tailored because fit is everything, and I needed to look put together and here for business. But I stressed less about nails and hair, gained signature traits, including statement glasses and bold lipstick. I stand out in the room because I don't look like everyone else; people see me.

If dramatic nails are your signature, go for it. Do you have a favorite color? Own it. I knew one woman who, under all circumstances, always had the best shoes in the room. You may have to think of this person you dress up as your alter ego, exuding confidence when you internally lack it. With practice, it becomes more and more comfortable.

People say, "I love leggings and sweats." Luckily, the "Clark Kent" version of you can wear those all day. Ultimately, I am talking about creating the most elevated version of you that you are comfortable with. There are many designers now who can make you look like you mean business while being completely comfortable.

You will see many people in the room who look the same and some with a very unique style. Chances are, it was a bit of an evolution, but one they are now known for. It could be the multi-millionaire in the tracksuit, the person with the high-end tailored suits with high-end sneakers, or the person who always wears leather pants. These people know the requirements, have done the homework, and can show up with their own definition of flair. That is the goal, to be so recognizable that people know you when you walk in, and know that you are suited up for the game.

Become your own emoji

Steve Jobs had a look. Anyone could walk around in a black turtleneck and blue jeans on Halloween, and we would know who they were dressed as. Find your look in something timeless, and don't jump from trend to trend unless it is a minor adjustment. The idea is that if you have a "look," you will be easily recognized. This is good because (1) people love it when they are in a room and recognize someone, (2) you won't have to keep reminding people who you are (trust me, it's a time-saver), and (3) it makes it very easy to get ready for appearances.

Clothing is available at different prices, ranging from the top-of-the-line to thrift stores. What is most important is knowing what colors you look good in and what shapes work best for your shape. Avoid trends if they do not look good on you. Contact a professional if you need some advice. Again, most major department stores have stylists, and some work independently.

Know what looks best on you and gather new uniforms based on fit. Try sizing up if your size feels a little tight. The thought hurts, but since actual sizes are impossible in women's wear, different designers may define your size differently. If you find a brand that works well, know that your entire uniform may come from that designer.

Our hair, our crowns, and our true personality are always sticking points. When I started, I tried to match the room, but I had more confidence when I wore my hair in a way that made it look the most natural. I stopped worrying if it was all in place and knew that this curly, sometimes frizzy, mop was my signature.[89] Decide if your natural hair is an option.

Asking a professional hair stylist for help could be key to getting easy-functioning hair. Find a stylist who understands your hair. If you like someone else's hair, ask where they get it done. You may need highlights, lowlights, or layers, but have them work with the hair you have been given. Women have been expected to put a lot of time and money into their hair. Shoot for a look that is all you.

Some people still might battle you on what is considered "professional" hair. I hate that term because your hair just grows out of your head with a mind of its own. The bottom line is that how you wear your hair has little to do with how awesome you are.

Shoes. Dress for comfort. Period. There are so many styles to pick from, and they can be your signature too. Comfort comes in all shapes. Some women are comfortable in high heels, and others are comfortable in athletic shoes. Whatever you choose, make sure they are well cared for and look stylish. Every style of shoe has an elevated look; shoot for that target.[90] The objective is to look like a player.[91]

---

[89] *Something that an athlete is known for to such an extent that it is hard to imagine another athlete doing it.*

[90] *An area used to score points or achieve objectives.*

[91] *A person that is skilled at a game.*

Personally, I like a shoe with a little stacking so I can look my fellow players in the eye, or at least close enough.

All that is left to discuss is personality in the personal branding journey. Think about your brain team again. How would the brain team want this alter ego, business you, "future you" to behave? It's all you, don't worry. They are now all going to be given a chance to speak.

Start by thinking about who is in charge right now. Is it the personality that holds the impostor syndrome or the personality that just keeps their head down and works? Is it one that is only living in the moment without any planning or the one that is so compassionate that it gets walked all over? It is probably a combination of a couple of personalities, knowing that one might have to step up and take the shot.

HUDDLE When building your personal brand, it helps to know your values. What do you want to be admired for or admire in other people? I value honesty, responsibility, drive, and creativity, and this is what I want to be known for.

Make a list of values that are near and dear to you. Revisit your "why" from Simon Sinek's book *Find Your Why*, and find your strengths and superpowers. It is really important to explore this because you may be completely off track.[92] No real growth can happen if you are in a place that does not excite you or feed your soul in some way. If you are not there now, do not worry because you have gained a lot of experience up until now,

---

[92] *Away from the racetrack, or not happening where a race is being held.*

and you can switch gears to get back on your path once you know where your power is.

Going forward, know that this is what you stand for. Can it change? Heck, yes! I think that I have reinvented myself at least five times. That is the best part of growing and changing. You will be exposed to more and more incredible things, and opportunities will arise, and what you stand for and what you want to be an expert in will evolve along with you.

Tell the brain team everything you know about your look, your values, and your why. Ask them how this person is going to walk into the room, how they will act in a meeting, how they will make a presentation, how they will speak up for themselves, and whether they will have the power to interrupt someone or speak up to make a point. Train yourself to listen to your voices of logic and reason, not always the ones with emotion. The more you practice these behaviors, the more they become comfortable.

Once this is all lined up, step into those shoes and own this elevated brand of you.

RULE #4: YOU NEED TO KNOW YOUR BEST POSITION ON THE FIELD

You should never stay at the same level. Always push yourself to the next.

—Marnelli Dimzon, Filipina football coach and former player

A lot of people do not know what position they are best suited for when it comes to playing the game of business. Typically, we get into a career that we fall into and pick up a lot of responsibilities along the way. But what are we really good at?

Luckily, there are ways to find out. Let's start with determining our "Zone of Genius." The term "Zone of Genius" originated with Gay Hendricks in his book *The Big Leap*. In that book, he describes it as always working in a space that you are incredibly good at. For example, I am great at marketing, on boards, networking, and running a business. I am not great at spreadsheets, long math equations, or firing people.

Can I do all of these things? Sure. But I am not great at them and should probably hire someone to do them. If you try to get better at only what you are bad at, you will only be miserable. Stick to what you are good at, and you will excel.

From a business standpoint, you can also determine what you are really good at by identifying what you love to do. What can you be doing or working on and the time just evaporates? Discovering what you love doing and are good at means only focusing on those things to get you higher. It is like going "all in" on an investment that you know is going to take off.

Your strengths are your place for growth. Move past everything else when you can. Think of those strengths, those passions, and jump on it whenever you see an opportunity reveal itself. These strengths can point you in the right direction regarding where to take your career or business.

Sometimes, our careers take on a life of their own early because we have always known what direction we are going in. Sometimes we get deep in our careers and wonder how in the world we got here because we currently don't really like what we are doing. But now that we have identified ourselves better, we can take everything we have learned up until this point to redirect ourselves to our "Zone of Genius."

For example, I fell into a career in marketing because I interviewed for a job where I was the only candidate who knew how to use a Macintosh computer. I did have some marketing experience, too, and grew into that marketing and advertising role. I kept focusing on finding greater opportunities to work with the best people. I continued to climb and started working for Fortune 100 companies where I learned more about budgets, strategies, and discipline.

Working on freelance projects taught me even more about business, and when I was ready to step into being a founder of a staffing and recruiting company, I knew all of the essentials. I knew how to market, make budgets, build strategies, find work in marketing, sell, negotiate, and more. There was an entire piece of staffing that I really didn't have a lot of experience with, but that is where I added more education. It was a weird and wonderful career path that involved gathering experience, jumping at opportunities, and getting really comfortable with the idea that I was a CEO. I had found my zone.[93]

Before the idea of this book, people wanted to know what it was that I did differently to get ahead. After some consideration, I realized that I had always made things. While my career detoured into a much more lucrative field of marketing, I never let go of the thinking needed to obtain that Bachelor of Fine Arts. Creating marketing campaigns and building store displays and signage were a part of my journey, and then marketing my own business while renovating homes, baking, writing, etc., fed my "Zone of Genius" and my strengths. I was basically problem-solving all of the time.

---

[93] *In sports, "the zone" refers to a mental state of peak performance where athletes achieve their best skills effortlessly and feel fully engaged in the activity.*

I talked to other successful people about this and then realized there was a pattern to this thinking. I then created a podcast called *The Secret Art of Business* where I have asked over a hundred entrepreneurs and business leaders three simple questions. One of those questions is, "What did you do as a child for fun?" And by that, I mean, what did you want to do before you had any responsibility? That thing that you gravitated to is your passion. I touched upon this in the last chapter about how this spark, this thread, will propel you forward if you identify it. The people who put on performances as children are now accomplished keynote speakers as adults. One leader I spoke with loved pickup games[94] of baseball, and he ended up building and leading winning teams. Another example is the person on my podcast who simply loved hanging out with friends in the neighborhood, and her favorite part of her job is networking and building relationships. That child who liked to play teacher is now a business coach.

HUDDLE I am asking you the same question. What did you do before you had any responsibility or commitments, when you were free to do what you wanted? If you couldn't determine it earlier, don't be disheartened; it might have been a while since you thought or felt that way. Some of the recurring things I heard were:
- Played outside with friends
- Organized tea parties
- Performed for the family

[94] A pickup game is a casual, unscheduled game of sports that's started by a group of players.

- Built worlds with Legos
- Read books
- Practiced drawing
- Played an instrument

Find the thread that starts with what your pure passion was and link it to what you can do now. This passion will be the fuel for your success. Make the time to invest in yourself and really unplug because when you come back to work, everything looks different and you are completely recharged. Does it work? Keeping it very simple, when we get really stressed, we need to take a walk. We develop our best ideas in the shower. When we want to "unwind," we need to activate our taste buds with food or wine. Imagine if you could go deeper with more things like this. Shut off that left brain for a while and let the right brain conjure up some brilliance based on a true passion.

Gift yourself the time to identify what it was that you loved doing and how it would make you feel. This is the seed that will grow into abundance. If the thread gets a little tangled—for example, you have an accounting firm and you love to bake—then bake. It works your muscles of problem-solving, creativity, and innovation, and with those new strong muscles, you will be able to tackle your job with more brain power. And your clients and your team will also appreciate all of the baked goods you bring in.

DELEGATE THE SMALL STUFF SO YOU CAN MAKE THE BIG PLAYS

Like most CEOs, when asked what they love to do, they answered, "work." Building a business and helping people and everything that goes with it is a constant learning experience. Great answer, right? It is all entirely true, but that alone was not the recipe for effectively building a career. Thousands of business owners spend time in their businesses. Still, few identify precisely what will get them farther, and discovering innovation and creativity provides unlimited fuel, reiterating that engaging your right-brain energy and your passion is the key thing that game-changers are using to elevate. For CEOs, this is delegating and eliminating everything else from the task list and focusing only on CEO activities because your innovative problem-solving skills will be needed.

CEOs and leaders can be responsible for endless things, but that doesn't mean they are caught up in the minutiae. They have teams to do the day-to-day work so that they can lead, create, and grow the business. For example, a CEO is going to have an overall knowledge of human resources, payroll, candidate reviews, marketing, etc., based on having experienced most of it firsthand, but they are not involved in the day-to-day problem-solving of it.

The CEO is the one who leads with the most passion about the company and the team. They are the ones team members look toward for the big answers, the big rescues, whole-brained thinking, and, therefore, coming up with the next excellent plan to move the business forward. This includes having time to do CEO tasks such as networking, business planning, closing the big contract, big-picture marketing, blog writing, and other elevated tasks.

Determine if you should be doing a task by how much the salary would be for that role. Are you paying yourself the owner's salary or at the pay scale reserved for the bat boy?[95] I handled a lot of the small stuff for years before delegating it all away. It was challenging to delegate because some of it was rather fun, and early on I didn't understand why I would pay someone to do these things if it only took me a minute, thirty minutes, an hour, two hours to do it. I would take the time to do it, even if it took time away from growing the business, even if it took time away from my family, even if it meant that I was paying my CEO, me, to print and mail out invoices. Delegating small tasks away not only provides opportunities to other people, but it also allows you to do what the CEO should be doing. You are hopefully paying yourself like a CEO. And if you are stuck in the business doing mundane things rather than doing your CEO duties, you are stealing from your own business.

Now, when tasks arise, I take on the responsibilities for things on my strengths list, that I have a passion for, and that should be owned by the CEO, and know that this combination is where my power is.

How did I delegate it? I told my team that I was no longer attending every meeting and no longer doing a specific task; I was granting them ownership of it. The surprising part was that they were happy for the opportunity and happy I

---

[95] *In the context of baseball, a "bat boy" or "bat girl" is a young person who assists at games by carrying bats, handling other equipment, and sometimes bringing baseballs to the umpire. They typically start with a pay rate at about minimum wage.*

was out of their hair. I was slightly sad that it was so easy. But that feeling was short-lived as I could now focus on the things that could build momentum.

STAY CURIOUS, BE CREATIVE, KEEP LEARNING

Don't give up on passions that are not directly connected to our current roles. They need to be incorporated into our lives in a different way; remember, we have to keep those right-brained sparks strong. You will find the time too. If you liked those performances as a child and you are incorporating speaking engagements into your career, look into local theater. If that Easy-Bake oven filled your days as a child, look into baking at home, taking a baking class, or holding all of your coffee meetings at a bakery. Some people were heavy into sports as a youth, and you can reengage in that by seeing if there are teams for that same sport as an adult, or explore options like pickleball, rowing groups, swimming, cycling, dancing, running, or taking some golf lessons. You can invite colleagues, potential clients, or team members to sporting events. Even going to the gym and focusing on the weights can be liberating when you reach new goals.

For example, I got back into painting, my true calling, after years of hiatus. It was literally lost for a while because businesses do not need many fine art painters. But the concept of allowing myself to operate in a space of a passion that I have, to do a right-brained activity, gave me the break I needed to conquer whatever I had left on my list.

This works for everyone. When fully immersed in a creative project, you walk away from the two hardworking left-brain characters living there. We give them a break, and that break is the key.

Millions of people deal with sadness daily because they do not walk away from the voices that tell them to keep working and keep trying harder. Working all the time is depressing and will get you nowhere because you are using only half your brain. The National Library of Medicine conducted a study that concluded that working long hours is a risk factor for the development of depressive and anxiety symptoms in women. Stop working harder and start working smarter.

Do you need a plan to stop the cycle of work? Most of us are slaves to our calendars, so lean into that discipline and schedule time to work on your creative side. If you haven't already, start with scheduling everything in your personal life, every appointment from the doctor to the car tune-up, and make it private on the company calendar. Then, add time for unplugging the left side of your brain to the calendar and keep the commitment. Give yourself fifteen minutes between meetings to take a walk, thirty minutes to read, a half day on Friday to paint, two hours to go to a museum, and time to journal, write poetry, and more as long as it is all for you and all activities that spark your innovation.

If you are still struggling to reignite your creativity and innovative skills, here are ten things that may provide a spark. They range in time commitment, so you can start slowly if you need to.

1. *Take a walk with no music* and really listen to the sounds around you.

2. *Take a walk and bring your phone because we are going to use that camera.* Look around at all of the details around you and take pictures. Use the portrait filter if you have one to make them look a little more snazzy. Don't judge yourself because the idea is to take time to be quiet and look. Get up close to see the detail; try shots from different angles and perspectives.

3. *Put on THE SONG that makes you tap your feet,* wiggle a bit, or completely want to dance. You might have to look back to your clubbing or college days, but there is that one song.

4. *Put on THE SONG that makes you want to sing along* so loudly that you almost drown out the singer who recorded it. Sing another one.

5. *Make a dish from scratch.* Find a recipe, get the ingredients, and figure out how to make it. Did you ruin it? Okay, it's not your dish. Find another one and nail it!

6. *Make a dish from a box.* Hey, we are not all made to do complicated dishes. Sometimes, just adding two eggs and water is enough of a stretch.

7. *Try a new restaurant.* If #5 and #6 had no appeal or were a failure, this counts too! Our sense of taste can completely get us out of our heads if we challenge it. Try a new place and a new taste. It has to be new because a hundred potato chips will not

trigger creativity. We know what chips taste like, and that is just eating.

8. *Crafting.* Walk around your local craft store and see what you think you would like to attempt. Knitting, crocheting, painting, there are literally thousands of ideas at the craft store.

9. *The hardware store.* Making things doesn't have to be arts and crafts. You can tick things off your to-do list, too, like finally hanging that picture, repairing that nail hole in the wall, or finally starting that big project. The hardware store also has mulch and plants, and gardening is a huge creative outlet, so get those hands dirty!

10. *Last on my starter list, but the list could go on and on, is seeing what children are doing.* Childhood activities are the purest activities because they are conducted with no worries about time or responsibility. You can play with children, or you can build that Lego set on your own. You can get adult coloring books and that 64-box of crayons all for yourself. Get some Play-Doh and escape with the smell alone. A few other thoughts are game nights, movies that make you laugh, riding your bike around the neighborhood, and staying out until the street lights come on.

Our brains are a part of our body, and our body needs recovery time. If you have ever trained for a run, lifted weights for strength, or spent the day raking the yard, you know that recovery is just as important as the exercise itself. Let the working side of your brain recover because doing more of the same thing you have always done is not going to change things. Your vision needs to change, and that comes with thinking differently.

WHISTLE! Not having a creative mind or mindset can block opportunities because we simply don't see them. We look past chances to work with huge clients, accept invitations to to events, because we think that they are not for us. Our Left-Brained Emotional voice convinces us of these things. With a stronger Right-Brained Thinking and Emotional side, we become more aware of opportunities, see them becoming reality, and create a map to get there.

Working in our passion, our "Zone of Genius," our strengths, helps us create a vision of where we can see ourselves. For most of us, "a hard day's work" is successful. You work hard, cash your check, and repeat this until you die. This thinking has existed forever, so many cannot visualize anything bigger unless they try to work even harder. Breaking patterns and beliefs can cause the shift, and having this kind of grit can get you to where you want to go.

This is how some bad habits and addictions start as well. We are looking for an escape from our trapped lives, the repetition, so we get lost with things online, drink too much, overeat, and binge-watch reality shows because of our natural need to deactivate that side of our brain. Sometimes, it is a matter of giving ourselves permission to "get off the clock" and accepting that we have talents other than working hard.

When I was young, I drew for hours at a time. My fifth-grade teacher told me I was an artist. Game-changer! That was all that I needed to get started down a path of creativity. We sometimes wait for permission to make a change. And keep in mind that being exceptional at drawing, for example, doesn't define an artist or a creative person. I think it was two students in the fifth grade who were told they were artists and encouraged to keep drawing. The truth is, we are all creative in some way. We draw, paint, write, sew, garden, cook, bake, dance, play an instrument, tell jokes, build, decorate, and a list of other things that we have made into our own art form.

Someone gave me permission to do something that I loved. Consider this sentence your permission to take the time to do something that you love.

HUDDLE The key to reaching your vision is returning to your core passion and allowing yourself to spend time where this fuels everything.

Take a minute to think about these questions:

1. *What did I love to do as a child?* It makes zero difference if it can be connected to your current work. For example, if you love dancing, start dancing again, even if it is in your kitchen. Doing a right-brained activity, an activity connected to no responsibility, will help you

rediscover yourself. That action will fire you up to get back to work.

2. *Who was the person who recognized your talent,* gave you permission, or opened a door for you to do something that you loved doing?

3. *Now that you are an adult, what door do you want to open on your own?* What do you want to give yourself permission to do? Do you see someone in your life who is waiting for permission to take a big leap?

People may need to live in the grind in order to get things done, and people may not have the opportunity to incorporate that talent into their day-to-day life. I challenge you to find the time. A long to-do list should not stop you from your own personal growth. I know successful people who do this. For example, I know a woman with an amazing, decades-old company who must ride a roller coaster every few months. She will travel to do so. There is another successful woman I know who dances competitively. Another plays pickleball, one knits, and another has vegetable gardens. So, being respectful to your brain team and knowing that you have some great skills to offer in business, what passion are you feeding?

You are running a business or you are a parent and think there is no time for fun and games. But you have to find the time. You have to control your calendar in order to run more efficiently. If you don't, you keep running in place.

So, if you are currently living in a joyless spiral, know that it can be temporary.

We have all had times in our lives where joy seems to evade us. Take the leap when you see the chance to jump out of it, even for five minutes. If you have a crew to take care of, take the kids for a walk. Put on their favorite music and sing along. Throw them all in the car, drive to a new park, and pick up something for breakfast or dessert. Sit with them and play a game. Watch a show together. And don't take your phone; be engaged. They want to see your beautiful, expressive face. Kids especially know how to play and lose track of time. Remember how to do that with them. You are stealing minutes[96] at times, but in the end, it is worth it.

If you are a caregiver to an adult, find someone to help you. It may be hard to convince yourself that someone can do better, but we are not looking for better, just good enough to last an hour or a day. If that isn't an option, add a break in a different way. Maybe there is a card game they would love to play with you, or maybe you could put on some music from their youth. Music works magic with just about everyone and can be especially beneficial when we age.

Time can escape us and sometimes in the most ridiculous ways. Recently, I heard that with the time we spent scrolling or answering endless emails, we could have had a great workout, started that book, and challenged ourselves in the kitchen. Become hyperaware of the things that steal your time. It is time that you will not get back,

---

[96] *This refers to the strategic effort to gain additional time on the clock without the other team's permission, potentially leading to more scoring opportunities or delaying a crucial scoring play. Time is our most precious commodity; don't let work have all of it.*

and you could have spent it on something to make your life full. Getting caught up in it is so easy because we just want to escape. Why? Because our left brain desperately wants to turn off. Feed the right side and feed your passion.

GOING "ALL IN" AND GETTING OUR HANDS DIRTY

Start building even if it sounds absurd because every great building needs a cornerstone, every great building needs to start somewhere with a plan, and I will go ahead and say it, every great team starts with a rebuilding year. So today, you are either putting down that first brick or building on what you have started.

When I was in my building stage, I was bussing and waiting tables, and I was at that factory job during summer hours. It was not the final destination that I saw for myself, but these jobs taught me a ton of things. I could have jumped off at any of those stages of building, but it didn't feel like I was where I needed to be, so I built more. Every step was knowledge and experience that I used as leverage to build the next story.

> **Follow your heart and find your soul.**

Where are you in your build? And before you say that it is too late to add more, it isn't. People change direction in their careers all the time. Rather than getting tied to your college degree or the years that you have invested into your career so far doing one thing, look at it as the blocks you need to place to launch your next thing. Many people have started their next thing over age fifty, sixty, or older. You have the time. Every step to get to your end zone[97] is based on the blocks that you are building with, and that can happen at any time. Up until now, everything you have learned or experienced may be all the tools needed to be that award-winning CEO, board member, public speaker, or author.

Your place on the field can only be fully achieved if you embrace all of your accomplishments and own every brick. Too often, women start businesses that are the same job they did for someone else. I hear women talk about their companies in a way that may make them think they are humble, but it translates into a business that cannot take on the big jobs.

- *"It is just me."*
- *"I have this small business."*
- *"I own a little boutique company that specializes in ..."*

Humility will get you nowhere, sweetheart. Even if your business is just you, speak about it as if it were bigger. Try these instead:

- *"My company solves problems for ..."*
- *"Hello, I am the President of ABC Company, and we ..."*
- *"I am the CEO of a company that specializes in ..."*

---

[97] *The end of the field where, if you have the ball, you score for your team.*

> **Don't downplay your accomplishments. You have worked hard. We tend to downplay our accomplishments to make others feel comfortable or because we are afraid that we have reached our limit.**

Self-sabotage is rampant among women. Society already likes to keep us in a box. There is no need for us to add the lid. Speaking about the facts of your accomplishments should give you more freedom to speak about them in a group. It is not bragging if you are just stating facts. I am not saying to be a bore, but own your accomplishments. Do you know who owns their accomplishments? Men. Men like to puff up and compare, um, resumes. This is the game. Show that you can play. Be chosen for the team because you are skilled, strong, and know what you are doing.

Have the vision.

Add the brick.

The game doesn't end until you quit. Until then, keep plotting ways to grow personally, professionally, and in areas that make you a little fearful. Challenge yourself. Is there a board you would love to be on because you know you could make a difference? Be bold and take a chance. Chances are, you meet all the criteria and just need to ask. Another way on a board is if someone on that board can be your champion and get you considered. Volunteer boards are always looking for help; it is a great place to start serving.

Add the brick.

Don't underestimate your own story either. Based on your very own story, are there speaking engagements you could do that would help others learn from you or see themselves in you? Public speaking is a fantastic way to be heard, noticed, and seen as an expert. It could also reactivate your love of performing. We would like to hear from you if you are an expert. Storm that stage!

You might love writing over public speaking and are ideal for writing articles, blogs, or other content. This is also a great way to be seen as an expert and to get followers. Once you have that, you can start moving up the roster.[98] As an expert, you will be the person people will go to when they need your expertise. You might think that a man will just hire another man's company. That is not always true. Men like to win and pick the players to help them win.

Add the brick.

Do women want to win? Some women just want to get along, get by, give back, and take whatever is left over for them. The evidence is all around us. That approach is a choice, but you can still grow by adding a few things. If giving back is your thing, then growing financially and in expertise means that you can give back more.

Add the brick and keep building.

> **Knowing your position on the field, what you are good at, and what will make you thrive is powerful. Accept the challenge and adjust your life to fulfill that destiny.**

THE POWER OF MONEY

Many people are now talking about a money mindset. A money mindset is a person's beliefs and attitudes about

---

[98] *The list of players that make the team. Moving up the roster means that you are a better player as they are ranked by skill.*

money, which cause mental blocks that can affect their financial decisions and behaviors. How do you really feel about money? When you were raised, maybe money was "the root of all evil" or "money doesn't grow on trees." Maybe you were taught that the life of poverty was the pathway to salvation. You could also have been raised where "greed is good," and the size of a person was measured by the size of their wallet.

Things that can occur and you may be experiencing:

1. You hold back from being in the same room as champions. You think that you don't deserve to be there.
2. You only grow so much so that you and others don't feel uncomfortable.
3. You can't grasp the idea of being wealthy, only going from month to month with money, even if it comes at the risk of your future comfort.
4. You struggle to break free of your comfort zone from those childhood thoughts.
5. You self-sabotage by overspending, binge-spending, and buying things you don't need in order to soothe those left-brained voices.

Guess what? You can have everything you want. You can save money and you can buy nice things. You can live fully in your accomplishments and make yourself and other women proud of you. Men will also see you as the player they want on their team. It's all win-win!

This may all come with a catch because with growth comes money, and money in marriages and partnerships is sometimes harder to navigate. Some people we partner with do not want to take a second seat to being the "breadwinner." Being taken care of is great, but being able to take care of yourself is better. You need to determine if this is an issue in your relationship, and if it is, can that relationship be rewired for you to be accepted as a high achiever and to grow? Determine if you are living with your Left-Brained Emotional Character that not only wants to protect you, but does it in a way that stops your growth.

Friendships and relationships with family are also very tricky. We all have our tribes, and no one wants to see someone leave the tribe. If you are surrounded by the best people, they will only be thrilled when you find your path. They may ask for help in finding their path too.

Before your mind explodes, hear me out—you owe it to yourself to live up to your greatest potential. If someone makes you feel bad about that, they are not your friend, loved one, or champion. We can phase in and out of these relationships as we navigate this journey. Our true champions stay, and they cheer us on.

Control the time of the people trying to control you.

Another catch is that you will not always be available to everyone. Prioritize the things that need to be done on your path. Your biggest supporters receive the most of your time, while everyone else gets less. Invest time in the things that level you up, knowing that you will need the time to create and to fuel it.

Not everyone is going to evolve with you. Control the relationships; when the time comes, you can weave them back where you can.

One last thing: Even when you are becoming fully formed as a business leader, you still may be playing two different roles. There is "off-duty" you and "badass executive" you. Be comfortable with both because sometimes you run into another CEO at the home improvement store, and sometimes you are called "fancy pants" by the people you grew up with. Take no offense. They are just seeing the entire person that you are.

RULE #5: BEING YOUR OWN AGENT MAKES BIG SHIFTS

You've got to be confident when you're competing. You've got to be a beast.

—Gabby Douglas, the first African-American gymnast to win an Olympic individual all-around gold medal

Successful sports figures have coaches and agents.[99] I have been my own agent for years, meaning that I have negotiated my own salaries, done my own promotion, and had to tell everyone about myself. You can, too, because no one knows you better than you.

---

[99] The person that makes the deals, negotiates the money, and gets their client in the room. Celebrities have these for the same reason. You are awesome; tell your story.

With my background in marketing, it was easy, especially when I thought of myself in the third person or as the person I was promoting. It is a bit of a mind twist, but it works. Keep problem-solving the question, "How can I get this product into your cart?" The product, of course, is you and the help or knowledge you bring. It could be just as easy for you because you know how to promote your child, partner, or best friend. Now just do it for you.

When the doors opened in my business, my first thought was, how can I promote what we are doing, and where do other business owners get their information? Our first plan was to get an announcement in the business newspaper. Why not an ad? We didn't have money for an ad, but the story of starting a business is free. The strategy was that all reporters want a great story; their job was to tell stories, so give them something interesting. For this, we go back to our story and our "why." When meeting the reporter, I needed to be a great agent for us and not hold back on what we could do and what we wanted to accomplish.

So, as your agent, you must tell your story very proudly. At times, we want to be humble, but this is the time to try and take the shot.[100] Our story was about two former corporate employees setting out on a new adventure in staffing for creative people. At the time, this was the first time anyone in our community was doing this specific type of recruiting. It made for an interesting quarter of a page story and got us "in the room" with people who own businesses. We were now known to the community, right? No, but it was a fantastic start, and I quickly found the

---

[100] *When you have an open opportunity to score in a game TAKE THE SHOT! And the crowd goes wild!*

rhythm of how being my own agent and my company's agent could work.

One of the things I was driven to do was to get back into the corporate headquarters we just left—as their vendor. I had to become the agent that went in and worked to get a "champion" on the inside. Once the conversation was started, it was my job to continue to sell our service up the food chain.

- *"We understand what you need."*
- *"We were you, so we understand the roles needed."*
- *"We can make this work for you."*

I was relentless because I was so sure we could do this job and do it well. Even though it was two people asking to work with a Fortune 100 company, we only presented ourselves as a major player in what they needed. That audacity came from seeing the vision so clearly.

We got in and grew exponentially.

Have the audacity to dream bigger.

My next job as my agent was to expand upon this story. I wanted to physically get in the room with other business owners by attending many, many events. Following my earlier rules, I made a power pose for a few minutes, walked into the room like I owned it, took a deep breath, and got ready to shake some hands.

I started with a hello to some acquaintances and asked a lot of questions. Then I took a minute to look for someone of influence and introduced myself. Then I listened and responded. Remember, it sometimes turns into a conversation, sometimes not; it's okay either way because you have met. The strategy is always to learn about people and see how you can help them, not to be in full sales mode. Only come in as a solver of problems. Everyone is taking time out of their day to be there, so be respectful. If there was a program or presentation affiliated with this event, I sat in a place where I would be seen. And you, your agent, will thank you because being seen, recognized, and adored are a part of the job, so do the work.

Adjust your story for brevity. Have a one-sentence version and a longer one. Stick with it and put it into action. When you are out networking and someone asks what you do, unleash the short story to build some interest. Have the entire story on deck[101] for the right moment with the right connection.

With my coaching business, my mini elevator pitch to gain interest is, "Do you know how women feel frustrated with getting ahead in business? I can help them fix that." With a setup like that, how can they not ask more questions?

HUDDLE The opening line for any networking situation is easy. Break down what you do into the simplest form.

- *Identify the pain point that your business addresses.*
- *Then say that you fix that.*

---

[101] *This generally means ready and waiting to act; literally in a baseball context, it is the next batter in line.*

Here are some examples:

- *For recruiting: "What do I do? Do you know how companies struggle with finding great talent? I take that burden away from them."*
- *For accounting: "Do you know how business owners need to spend more time being owners? I effectively take away the task of accounting off their plate."*
- *For catering: "Putting on events can be a heavy lift, so I make sure a company's event is flawless and memorable."*
- *For T-shirt sales: "You know how T-shirts are sold everywhere? I sell shirts that are above the rest in quality and fit."*

Now it is your turn. Create a very simple two-line statement for what it is that you do: the pain point and the solution. Then, go try it out at the next event. If you don't get a response of any kind, you may need to rework it. It is effective even if the only response generates some questions for you because that means the message has been delivered and understood, and is much more memorable.

WE NEED TO ASK FOR MORE

Agents are great at negotiating your price to do business. Almost everyone has to be their own agent when it comes to negotiations, so let's talk about how you handle that. It starts with being brave enough to ask.

Men typically start with a higher price. Why not? If they start high, they can offer a generous discount and look like a good guy. The same thinking applies to salaries; they always ask for the top of the range. Are you brave enough to ask for what you're worth?

Women tend to have more issues with money than men. This comes from several sources, so let's address a few. When someone gets fouled or injured, we look for the referee, or "ref," when we see things occurring that are not fair.

W.E. - C. - R.E.F

W—WORTH

Women, more than men, do not see their own worth. We settle. We want to be helpful. We take whatever is given to us and are expected to be grateful. We are afraid to ask for more because we don't think we deserve it, because we think we are somehow burdening others by asking for more, or sometimes we don't know we can ask for more.

E—EVIL

Many people believe money is the "root of all evil." We hear that rich people are greedy and that money is more trouble than it is worth. I was raised believing that money is what others have, and we must know our place in society. As stated earlier, we all have a money mindset, and we need to figure out where we get blocked. It is not evil to want to be financially healthy.

C—COMFORTABLE

We get very comfortable in the familiar salary range. We choose to make it work in the same space we grew up in. We forget that getting out of our comfort zone is where growth happens. We nest and settle here. Women settle for the salary that feels good rather than the one we deserve. Check into what a person at your level in your area of the country should be making; you might be surprised.

R—RELATIONSHIPS

We are afraid to make more than our father, spouse, or partner because it may change the relationship dynamic. When we are programmed to have a male provider or a person in a relationship who is perceived as dominant, we step back if we start getting too successful. Believe it or not, some partners are not thrilled about our wins because it makes them feel less than us. Whether true or perceived, this is a situation many work with.

E—ENOUGH

We are conditioned to believe that there is a range of income in which we belong. We tell ourselves that we have "enough" rather than trying to push ourselves farther. Having more, going higher, creating a bigger company than we ever imagined can be scary because, for us, we have never played that game. It is like being a master of checkers and never trying chess. "I'm good. I'll stay right here. That game is too challenging." We stop our own growth by hiding in the "enough."

F—FRIENDS

Tension within our friend groups may start to appear as our status changes. Once, everyone could complain about their boss, but now you are a boss. If you get a new car or a bigger house and stop living the same way as the friends you have had for years, the dynamic changes. You may be afraid of losing friends.

WHISTLE! I am blowing the whistle here as a referee. Any time you undervalue yourself, it is a violation. Take a couple of minutes to think about whether or not you are making yourself the victim in this. Take another minute to ask yourself if you are being paid what you are worth.

Be relentless. You are fighting for you.

HUDDLE Make a list of things you still wish to accomplish in your career. Look at it from the perspective that you are the agent for you. What are some of your accomplishments that you are too humble to mention but a third party would say about you? Add bullet points for each of those items that begin to plot the course. The objective of this exercise is to start preparing you for that next level.

Be ready to get in the game and join a committee or board; participate in panel discussions, give keynotes, and contribute as a writer. We never know when an opportunity will come up, and we need to be ready. Keep an updated bio; it will save you a lot of time starting from scratch every single time.

Here are some tips and tricks when updating or creating your bio:

- *List all of your skills.* The key here is to think beyond your current position and include the other things you did in past jobs. Focus on skills that could be useful for the opportunity you are looking at. Some of this experience can be worked into a great cover letter or be part of the conversation. Think about skills you possess that would be a huge asset to a team, board, a committee, a panel discussion, or a presentation. Be prepared to showcase[102] those skills so everyone can see how you can support others.
- *Tell everyone you are looking for opportunities to share your experience and skills.* You are an expert, so tell all of your business acquaintances, anyone who has worked with you, and knows that you are the quarterback[103] in any situation. More people on the hunt for you will produce a

---

[102] *Sports showcases are events where athletes demonstrate their skills in front of college coaches and professional scouts, serving as a crucial platform for recruiting and scouting, especially for high school players. Time to show your stuff!*

[103] *The quarterback in American football is the person who usually lines up behind the center, calls the signals, and directs the offensive play of the team. They're go-to person, the one that makes things happen.*

quicker outcome. You have connections.
Let them help you because people love to
help, so don't deny them this joy. Do the
same for others.

- *Always align your search with something that
  can be a move-up, more exposure, or both.*
  Ideally, you get both, but you can use them
  as leverage for your next position or client
  lead. You are an expert; use it to your
  advantage because you have something to
  offer. When people connect with you, be
  the all-star [104] that they talked about.
- *Price yourself properly if money is involved,
  or measure the value or experience you will
  gain if you are volunteering.* Not focusing
  on getting paid for your expertise is
  where women fall short in being able to
  save money or increase their assets. Your
  time is worth something. If it is volunteer
  work, determine what you are giving up
  in order to do something for free. Gaining
  experience has value. Using an experience
  to promote yourself has value. Beware of
  the pitfalls of this because people are always
  looking for free things. That only works if
  you get something you want in return.

> People can always ask for something for free, a discount, or
> for you to take less than you believe that you are worth. I
> mean, why not? The thing is, you don't have to say "yes."

If you still struggle with negotiating your pricing or
anything else, Casey Brown has an excellent TEDx talk on

---

[104] *A team or list of players representing the top performers from different teams within a league or region.*

the Internet and a book called *Fearless Pricing* that addresses getting paid what you are worth.

A good agent is looking out for your advancement and is always watching for that next opportunity. You need to know what you want and ask for it so that you get what you want.

As CEO of my own company, I had to be the one stepping forward to ask for what the company needed and wanted. I learned that I could talk to other CEOs about what they needed. It is a 50-50 relationship of you providing goods or services as expected or better and then getting paid fairly for your work. Be the agent that knows how to get the deal closed, even if it starts to get awkward.

One of my favorite agent stories is when I met a CEO who did not wish to discuss staffing. I changed it to another way I could help beyond helping them with staffing their team. "If you have good candidates who didn't get the role with you, could you pass them on to us? We would love to help them." As I walked away, he said, "Hey, my daughter is graduating with an art degree. Could you talk to her?"

Not only was it a yes, but I also made a new friend with that CEO, which will be useful in the future. This deal was about helping his daughter, and he would speak highly of us when I was not in the room. Deals can be found anywhere, and negotiation tactics are endless.

THE PAYOFF OF BEING AGILE

Practice jumping into conversations. You are there to be in the game and not be a spectator. The people at events and in meetings are your peers and colleagues, and you have something to contribute. If you fear completely making a mess of hopping into a conversation, you can stop talking and listen for a better opportunity. Challenge that voice in your head that is holding your tongue and ask, "What is the worst that could possibly happen? These are just people like me wanting to do business and to meet people." Make your inner agent happen and show people what you've got.

> **Be your best agent. Be hyperaware of opportunities that can move the ball[105] in your favor.**

What is the worst that can happen as you are self-promoting? Let's say that the worst thing happens. How would you handle it if you were among friends? How would someone in that group handle it if it happened to them? If your agent was standing right next to you, what would they say? In the past, I've acknowledged it, shook it off, maybe laughed, and continued with, "Well, that was embarrassing" or "I can't believe that just happened," and then quickly changed the subject to something of importance.

---

[105] *This generally refers to a player or team advancing the ball toward the opponent's goal or end zone, or keeping possession of the ball while avoiding the opposing team. Baby steps count.*

An error[106] is often forgotten quickly, and the game continues. Remember that part about making yourself memorable? That can apply here too!

WHISTLE! Be aware if you are constantly apologizing. Take a breath, and before you apologize, think about how the situation can be addressed; for example:

- *Instead of "Sorry I am late," say, "Thank you for waiting."*
- *Instead of "Sorry that I have to cancel," say, "Something came up and we need to reschedule."*
- *Instead of "Sorry to interrupt," say, "I need to interrupt you."*

Strong leaders have important things to say and do, and respect is gained if we do not always fall back on those gorgeous heels.

We are always conscious of when people try to trip us up.[107] We are doing our best, and then someone takes the opportunity to insult us, test our knowledge, make a sexist comment—all for a laugh or because they are threatened by our presence in the room. If you are stunned into a position of having no reply, say nothing. Cause an awkward pause

---

[106] *When someone makes a mistake during a baseball game. Missed throw, missed catch, etc.*

[107] *In sports, "tripping" refers to an illegal act where a player intentionally uses their body or equipment to disrupt an opponent's balance or cause them to fall, which is a penalty in most sports. It's a foul. And it really is foul. It typically comes in the form of critical words in the form of good humor. Don't fall for it.*

and let those comments deflate[108] right before you. Once the air is out, it is easier to handle.

Your agent would tell you to "walk it off"[109] quickly and get back in the game. Sometimes we don't need to say a word and just walk away, as other people in the room can determine if this is a decent person to work with.

> *Ways to let the air out of something said:*
> - *Say nothing. Just look them in the eye and say nothing. Pause and let the awkwardness of that comment hang in the air, and then say, "Anyway, I'm going to go." And go.*
> - *Laugh sarcastically. This also lets them know that their comment was ridiculous and did not harm you in any way.*
> - *Comment, "Wow, I am not sure how to respond to that."*

Unfortunately, how you respond will be how the confrontation is judged. You deserve to be in the room, in the conversation, because you have worked hard for it. Keep your poise and above all do not let that person take away your opportunity of being here.

Be aware that people will know if you are new or nervous, so try to mask all of that with the practices from earlier. Have some swagger. If you are immediately read as a non-player you will never be asked to join the game.

---

[108] *To reduce the internal pressure of a ball (by releasing the air) making it softer and potentially easier to grip, throw, or catch.*

[109] *In sports, "walk it off" generally refers to downplaying the severity of an injury and continuing to play or train despite pain, often with the implication that the injury is minor and will resolve itself. I swear, women have become pros at the art of "walking things off."*

You know many things, and not sharing what you know could be viewed as selfish.

You, as your agent, will want the world to know about your expertise beyond the room you are in. Start writing. Create newsletters, blogs, articles, or posts all in the area of your expertise. The world revolves around content and stories, and you have something to write about.

Find a platform where your clients and the people who need to know more about you are—the places that are a fit for what it is that you do. Do this enough, and people will start to recognize you and follow you. You will be seen as the expert in your field or part of your community. This is how you build credibility, trust, and a system of people being able to find you. This is how people choose you over your competitors. Do a minimum of two posts a week. Repurpose your content to appear on multiple platforms that your clients and peers visit. Choose something that you will be consistent with. Include photos or illustrations if possible, because this will make people spend a little more time with your post or blog. This is all self-promotion, and promoting you is exactly what an agent would do.

RULE #6: RUN ONTO THE FIELD LIKE YOU OWN IT

I don't run away from a challenge because I am afraid. Instead, I run towards it because the only way to escape fear is to trample it beneath your foot.

—Nadia Comăneci, five-time Olympic gold medalist

Your popularity is starting to set in. People are beginning to recognize you and know you are driven, intelligent, and great to be around. The next level is owning the room, meaning you are not wasting your time or anyone else's time when you enter. You are there to meet people and balance how you can be of service without giving away all of your time.

You have hustled, been strategic, quieted the overbearing voices, and can network with the best because you have already been tested. You are fully prepared to raise the bar for yourself and see how high you can jump. You are meeting people at a higher level because you can offer something. Do not deny people your skills, connections, and excellence in what you do. Do not let your impostor syndrome in the room because you have worked hard and deserve this. Sometimes you go to events to socialize and catch up with business friends, but make sure to have a strategy. My plan was two-part: strengthen existing relationships and meet someone new. So first, engage with friends.

Engaging with people you already know at an event always comes first. It serves as a good warm-up to conversing with others, and we want to create really solid relationships with people that we can have as cheerleaders[110] for us, and us for them. Meet with them all and be supportive of any news they have to report. Share the highlights of your life with them and see if there are any ways that you can support each other. It is these bonds that get us further.

Next are the people you don't know. Where do you start? If you are alone, you can go alone. If you are with someone, even someone you just met, take them along as a sidekick to meet people. Start with, "Let's go mingle. Do you want to meet X? Do you know them? We will now!" If you are networking by yourself, read on.

> ## Be interested and be interesting.

---

[110] *A member of a team that performs organized cheering, chanting, and dancing in support of a sports team. In business, it's the people that support us.*

Nothing works better in sales, relationships, and partnerships than face-to-face conversations, which is why you need to connect with as many faces as you can in a day. In Williams' book *The Connected Species*, he has a high-level discussion about how we need to see each other in person to connect. As humans, we need actual eye contact and the feeling of other people's presence.

So, even for a minute, connect with everyone you know, then move on to the ones that you don't know or have only met once. Feel free to skip the toxic people or the people who are not your cheerleaders. But real eye contact and being in each other's presence are key to making a true connection. Yes, virtual can be easier, but the results are better if we simply show up to an event. Science says so.

MAKING NEW FRIENDS

Making new friends at networking events is amazing. Look around the room and see who looks interesting, someone who would provide great conversation, and walk over with starter questions like these:

"Hi, I'm Catherine. What is your connection to the X Organization? Do you attend a lot of these events? What business are you in? How did you get into that? Tell me something that you really love doing in that field of work."

It is the plan that more conversation will organically grow from these questions.

WHISTLE! Don't make this an interrogation. Start with one question and think of a follow-up. Do a lot of listening. There's no talking about you yet, and don't start thinking of your answer while they talk. Listen with the intent of asking that follow-up question. This method does benefit you even when it is not all about you. Be genuinely interested in their responses so you can determine if this could be a future client or someone who can connect you to potential clients and opportunities.

Here's a quick bail, because not every conversation will bear fruit:

- *"Okay, I really need to go and get some coffee."*
- *"Listen, great talk, but I need to use the bathroom."*
- *Grab your phone. "Excuse me, I have to take this."*
- *"I need to run and say 'hi' to someone."*
- *Simply slip out, especially if a third person is in the conversation.*

In elevated conversations, you need to be engaged. This is pro-level. This is not a lightweight[111] conversation. It is a heavyweight.[112] Make eye contact, lean in to listen, mirror body language, and mix in conversational things rather than all business. Flipping from business topics to ones that

---

[111] *In boxing, rounds are decided by the weight of the boxer, the level they compete at. Lightweight is exactly that: typically less experienced but not always.*

[112] *In boxing, rounds are decided by the weight of the boxer, the level they compete at. Heavyweight is exactly that. These boxers are typically more experienced and have worked a lot on muscle mass.*

are simply conversational, fun, or trendy makes for a deeper connection.

Once you are at this level, you will build your personal team. This team goes beyond handshakes and sales and becomes champions, mentors, and confidants. The higher up the ladder you go, the more people you need to have near you that you can trust and that you can call on. These people are those you will rely on in your business world. This world has problems that can only be addressed by people in the same situation. Build that team for now and in the future. Your squad can be small or large, but consider it your personal or business advisory board.

Here is how you do that.

You have been networking for a while. Ask yourself, "Who have I really connected with? Who are the people in a similar field who can relate to what I am going through?" Talk to them now. Offer to meet people for coffee, tea, or a meal for deeper conversations. Networking events or meetings leave little time to get to know a person. The breakout conversations are where the real relationships are made.

Find a common thread. The very best relationships are when people find something they have in common. For women, it is easy because we can talk about being a woman in business and other business things. It can also be easy in mixed company, and we can talk about, wait for it, sports! Get a group of guys together, just throw out the team name, and let the conversation begin. It's the highest level of connection, and you can be in it. You don't have to know every trade[113] and play,[114] but it does help you learn something.

HUDDLE You will run into a lot of the same people at events because they, too, want to be in the game. These players are reliable and relatable, and can be the top tier of people you reach out to for advice and referrals. Because you have met numerous times, they really care about you and your business. Be available to these people as well. You can elevate these relationships into an advisory board if you want to carve out time for you all to get together to discuss specific topics.

If you choose to go in the direction of formal advisors or creating your own advisory board, make sure that everyone signs a non-disclosure agreement (NDA), also known as a confidentiality agreement, which is a legally binding contract where parties agree to keep certain information confidential. You can find a template for one on the Internet. My advisors would meet quarterly, and they were paid with a stipend and lunch. The group was composed of both men and women. I also had a separate group of people who were more at a social level. They were equally valuable as advisors, and because it was more casual and never about top-secret things, we didn't need NDAs. Build the team that you need.

---

[113] *Literally, when a player gets traded to another team.*
[114] *The movements a team makes to try to advance the ball down the field to score.*

WHISTLE! Sometimes, the communication with others is confused by some as flirting or looking for something other than business. It happens. Walk it back as quickly as you can.

- *"Oh my goodness, that is not what I meant."*
- *"I am currently in a relationship with someone I really care about."*
- *"I see that you took your shot there, but no."*

Keep the response quick, light, and not accusatory. And quickly move on. The idea is that regardless of whether the statement by the other person was flirty or foul, you don't want it to continue, and you don't want to embarrass the other person because that will gain you nothing. It will happen, and the more you treat it like it isn't a big deal, then it won't be. At this level, how you react is important. Everyone in the room is connected, and you need to have some control over the narrative. How you take control of the situation is how your character will be seen going forward.

If it becomes a big deal or a power play[115] because some people won't take "no" for an answer, walk away immediately to another person you know in the room. You are a strong, professional woman who doesn't have time for people who behave badly. Channel a strong woman you know and calculate how they would get out of this situation.

---

[115] *In ice hockey, a power play happens when one or two players from a team commit an infraction or a penalty. The team is immediately outnumbered. Which means the opposing team can make a move with more power.*

Enough talk about bad players. We can make some great connections and build relationships, but just don't forget that you will need to work the room again. Unless this last conversation is a high-power deal, it's time to break[116] away and find your next conversation. The best part is that you can get any person's information and continue the conversation over coffee or ask if they typically come to these events, because you will look for them next time. And do it, because in the formula of threes, after three conversations like this, you can consider them a go-to person for an ask.

This is a mountain we all must climb. Get your rope, helmet, harness, and crampons.[117] We are going up!

Every business leader has a following. Be the person others want to follow because you have exhibited yourself as bold, brave, interesting, smart, and connected. Ask for nothing yet, because it is not about asking for anything right now. We don't want the social disconnect, so the pitch[118] will come later. The idea behind this is that we do not want to sour a relationship by immediately trying to sell to someone. Everyone hates being sold to. It is the relationship that is vital. People want to work with other people they like and respect, and making any ask too soon and any opportunity for a relationship is lost.

> ### Introduce yourself, shake hands, and be delightful over and over again. Then, you get your break.

---

[116] *Immediately finish a conversation with a plan of action and get back to work.*

[117] *It's a metal plate with spikes fixed to a boot. Even saying the word "crampon" makes me think of other things.*

[118] *In baseball, a pitch is the act of throwing the ball toward home plate to start a play. The "ask."*

Always approach from a place of helping; people will work with people they like and respect. That second part takes a little more time, but it is worth it. Going too fast could mean shooting a brick[119] and a missed opportunity. Now hey, if they want to set up a meeting to work with you immediately...SCORE![120] You know what to do from here. Most of all, it is incredibly rewarding to just walk around a room, have delightful conversations, and help people.

Rejection is just redirection.

The time will come when you see your opening and are ready to make your pitch. It could be sooner than you think, so always be ready, especially if you have already offered to help someone in some way. Here is how I would sell my services; it all starts with some:

- *Friendly conversation.*
- *Great listening. Really listen to your potential client or connection for issues and needs.*
- *Tell them what you do in a way that piques interest: "You know how women struggle with getting ahead in leadership roles? I help them fix that."*
- *If they don't have a need, pivot to just staying connected, as in, "If you know of anyone who could use my services, please let me know," or "If you don't need my services now, that is okay, because at least*

---

[119] *A brick is a term that is used to describe a missed shot. It is also those giant, old mobile phones that I guess you could throw as well, but that is a different conversation.*

[120] *A team or player has successfully gained a point, goal, or other form of scoring in the game. It's a general expression of excitement and celebration when a team or player achieves a significant moment in the game.*

*we are connected, and we can tell others about what
we do."*

Sometimes it is simply rejection that happens. There are
a lot of reasons why you will get a "no," and none are personal
unless you came on too strong. Rejection comes when:

- *A person or company is happy with who they are
  using.*
- *They are comfortable enough with who they are using.*
- *It is complicated to change vendors.*
- *They are not the person who chooses the vendors.*
- *The fear of making a change and starting over with a
  vendor is an unknown experience.*

You might have more to prove to them, or you just won't
be working together. It is nothing personal. However, if they
see that you keep showing up, they know that you are in
the game. Maybe you can take them to lunch to understand
their needs and offer your services again. Ask if they can
bring the decision-maker or connect you to that person.
Meanwhile, they might recommend you to someone else,
which means it is a warm lead. How long you wish to try to
connect with someone is your choice, but always remember
that there are thousands of people out here, and you need
to find your people. Shuffle through the people you have
met and keep checking in. Timing is everything, and you
may catch them on a day they are a little more receptive or
their current vendor just made a huge mistake, giving you
an opportunity to step in. The best part is that you have
already met and had conversations, so you have created your

own warm lead. Constantly watch for openings and spaces where you can make your next move.

RULE #7: BIG CHANGE HAPPENS WITH CHAMPIONS AND CHEERLEADERS

Somebody gives you an opportunity, say yes to it. So what if you fail? You won't know if you fail or succeed unless you try.

—Ann Meyers, retired pro basketball player and sportscaster

Champions[121] and cheerleaders[122] are the best of the best relationships to have in business. These people know you and your work and are willing to tell others about you. Above all, if you can be either to anyone else, do it. It is an investment in your future.

---

[121] *The winners, the ones that have fought a long fight, know how to play the game the best.*

[122] *The people on the sideline that cheer the loudest for you or get others excited about you.*

Let's start with cheerleaders.

Cheerleaders, like those we typically see on the sidelines of American football games, are there to build up enthusiasm. GO! FIGHT! WIN! When we have people like this around us, it fuels our growth. When it comes to spouses and partners, you really need them as a support system, even if they have no connection to the work that you do. Parents and friends can also step into this role when you need someone to do the one thing you cannot get to.

> **Our cheerleaders don't pick us like flowers to be admired. They feed us what we need and let us grow.**

A cheerleader is someone who supports you with words or actions. Be one and make room for them. Some key phrases are:

- *"What can I do to help you?"*
- *"I am so proud of you."*
- *"It is so fun to watch you grow."*

Look for your cheerleaders and go to them when you need a boost or pep talk. Sometimes, the best pep talk can come from a stranger. Really listen when any of this happens.

HUDDLE If you are not sure of all of your superpowers, ask a cheerleader. They will see the things in you that you overlook and take for granted. Write out the things that people say about you and put them in a place where you can always look at them. You can take personality polls or read your horoscope, but get some starting points if there is no one to tell you, from a business standpoint, what you are good at. Once you are sure of what you are good at through conversations or testing, you can reference these strengths in conversations about what you can additionally offer the world beyond earned degrees or skills learned on the job.

Champions, on the other hand, can move mountains for you. These people can introduce you to the right people, get you on boards, and provide enormous leaps for you because they are already in the room that you want to be in or think you need to be in. I have had champions submit my name for committees and board roles, connect me to people that could use my company's services, and steer me through the choppy waters of business.

> **Have faith and believe in what a Champion sees in you.**

Champions are those who have worked with you and see something in you. They know that you show up, work hard, speak up, and get things done. You might already be a fit for a lot of things, but you didn't see your own talents.

WHISTLE! If someone opens a door for you, do not say no; walk through. When it comes to saying no, we are always determining whether we are ready to elevate, doing the math on whether or not we feel qualified. When someone sees something in us, take the chance that you will eventually see it too. Quiet the noise of your Left-Brained Emotional Character and think more about the possibilities. This is an opportunity to meet more leaders, exhibit what you are good at, and gain more experience. Don't underestimate how much people want to help you. Also, know that if you don't step up, that person will remember and might not ask you to step up again. Once you accept a role, make sure to do a great job and make that person proud of you. You will be seen as a reliable, smart go-getter and be invited to more tables and offered the next rung of the career ladder.

I was approached early in my CEO role to join the Small Business Council of my city's Chamber of Commerce. A woman who I met at several events told me that she was putting my name in for consideration. She actually could make it happen. The first words out of my mouth were something like, "I don't know if I am ready for that." It could have ended there, but lucky for me, she understood my hesitation and insisted. Actually, I think she had already submitted my name.

The lesson I learned here was to just throw your hat in the ring[123] and let their team decide if I am ready. They added me to the council and I met some of the most amazing business owners, many of whom I am friends with years later. Of course, she talked me into being the chair of that committee—that led to being on the Board of the Chamber,

---

[123] "Throwing your hat in the ring" is an idiom for accepting a challenge or entering a competition. Clearly men don't appreciate their clothes since they are throwing hats and gauntlets around.

where I was awarded for being in the same room as some of the top CEOs in the city. One champion shepherded me to a role that turned into a huge move. More on boards later.

WHISTLE! Champions are also the ones who can walk us into a client's office that we never thought we would get into. Sometimes, this is the only way it happens. Huge clients can be impenetrable. You need to have a person inside to open that door for you. One of the most prominent clients we had started precisely like this. It was a company for which we formerly worked. We knew what they needed and did a sales pitch based on that knowledge, but it was a person we knew on the inside who said to their people, "I want to use this company," and the game changed entirely in our favor.

Champions and cheerleaders are the people that we already know and the people we meet at the networking events. Those are the people who are doing business. You can have cheerleaders who are family and friends, but watch for saboteurs. The saboteurs are the ones who want you to stay like them, not grow up and leave the fold. You can stay back and indulge them, but it will cost you time, opportunities, and money. Be their best cheerleader for as long as possible, offer to help them grow, too, but fight for yourself. If you've got the magic, you need to share it.

THERE IS NO SHAME IN ASKING FOR HELP

When going on a journey such as this, finding a person who is a mentor is the next natural step, and it is not as simple as walking up to someone and asking if they can be your mentor. Even if this person is amazing to you, chances are, they are very busy. The biggest leaders in the business always have requests for mentorship, and most of those requests come from people they do not know. There simply isn't the time for them to invest in every person that asks, and especially in someone they know nothing about. It is similar to walking into a bank and asking for money. If they do not know you or whether or not you will be a good investment, they are not going to offer to help.

When looking for a mentor, the best place to start is to look at the people around you. The champions that we talked about might be an option, but it is always the people who really know you, the ones who know where you are going and typically have been where you want to go. Again, this is where making connections is so important.

Follow this format and know that you are committing to doing all of the work:

- *Set up a time to meet for coffee or lunch with a potential mentor. Schedule it during working hours because this is work and it won't be confused as a date.*
- *Provide them with the topics you wish to discuss in order for them to be prepared; it is not an opportunity to "pick their brain." Yuck.*
- *Send them an email to confirm the day before.*
- *Arrive early. They are doing you a favor, and you must not let them wait.*

- *Immediately offer to pay the check. Again, their time is valuable, and this is a small price to pay for their time.*
- *If you like, ask if they would be open to meeting again. And take the cues if they want to meet or are trying to avoid meeting again. If it is the latter, not a problem, it just wasn't a good fit. There are other people.*

Meetings like this can develop into a series of meetings where you both get to know each other. If you find someone who "clicks" with you, you can keep the relationship very informal, which may be easier for a person with little time. At these one-on-one conversations, ask for suggestions on books to read and places to go to make connections. Try what they suggest and report back with what happened. See if they can make an introduction for you.

This kind of casual mentorship is easy for everyone, and I added more than one mentor to my list this way. Some didn't even know that they were mentoring me; it was just lunch. What I liked about it was that I could get a variety of perspectives and have lunch with various amazing people. It works well when the people you want to talk to are unable to commit to a formal mentorship.

On the opposite end of the spectrum are the people who weigh us down and impede our growth. They are not our cheerleaders or our champions. We all have people in our lives who stress us out or peck us down a size. They don't support our dreams. They make us feel insecure. They make us feel like we can't do anything right.

You need to gradually phase those people out of your orbit. These people could be bad clients, poor employees, or adversaries on a board that we chose to be on. Know that the people you surround yourself with are just as important as working on your own self-growth. A flower can grow through a crack in the sidewalk, but it will flourish in a field of fellow flowers.

Finding your circle of people that energize you will take time. You are going into new rooms and making new connections. Ask those people where they are going, what they are reading, and who is inspiring them. This will open up a new world to you that you never knew existed.

Also, be very self-aware and be grateful. I have mentored some ladies who make me feel like it is my job to make them impactful. It isn't. Only you can do this job, and you really have to put the effort in. Never say things like:

- *"I've tried that."*
- *"I don't think that I am smart enough."*
- *"I didn't have the time to do what you told me."*
- *"I don't think that would work."*

If something like this comes up, talk it through. Your mentor cannot know everything you tried or absolutely everything about your company or what you are trying to accomplish. They are advisors and you still have to make the decisions and do the actual fixing. Having an attitude like this will quickly end a relationship, so be all in; otherwise you are out.[124]

---

[124] *When a player at bat or a base runner is retired by the team in the field. Or...you're done.*

RULE #8: THE BIG LEAGUES ARE READY WHEN YOU ARE

Celebrate the success of one woman as a collective success for all women.

—Abby Wambach, soccer player, coach, and member of the National Soccer Hall of Fame

Remember the stats I gave you earlier about women in business? We need to be cheerleaders and champions for our fellow women to succeed. Women on boards, in front of audiences, running businesses, and in leadership positions can only happen if we all work to make it happen. When asked to be in a meeting, event, board, or new position, don't be timid; you were asked to be there. Don't disappoint yourself and others.

It is at this time that fear and awkwardness will appear because the big league is uncharted waters for you. And like before, you will ask yourself questions like, "Do I belong here? Am I smart enough? Where should I sit? What can I expect? Where is the trash can for my empty coffee cup?"

These were some of the questions in my head for my first board meeting. I wanted to do a good job and impress people; the quickest way was to participate and dare to be brave and dare to be awkward. People like a little imperfection because it makes them feel comfortable with their own imperfection. The best boards that I have been on were when the members were open, honest, and collaborative. Be all of those things, even if you might have an opposing opinion or view. Boards are about problem-solving, debate, and discussion. All views are, or should be, welcome, and you have been asked here to share yours.

For your first meeting I can recommend that you go and simply listen and get a feel for the room. Figure out the group's dynamic and who is in charge, and determine who the big thinkers are and who you need to watch out for.

Paying attention is participation. Asking questions and offering suggestions is the next level. Play to the next level. Not every question is perfect, and not every suggestion is brilliant, but do it anyway. You were asked to play the game, not sit in the field and play with the grass. How well you participate shows others your value, and you will be asked to do other, more significant things. The Board Chair loves it when people participate by asking questions and offering suggestions or tweaks to an idea. Again, you were asked to be here.

- *Participate by asking clarifying questions, and challenge yourself to ask at least one good question at every meeting.*
- *Share the expertise that you have.*
- *Get there early and talk to people.*
- *Be a cheerleader and a champion for others.*

Do not remain in the background because that is more comfortable. Don't fall into the trap of "I'll just sit back here and observe or my attendance is enough." Ask yourself why you feel like you are not important enough to play in this game. Is it fear of failure or of making a mistake? I can promise you that the men are showing up and being heard without question. So should you. Be a part of being in the room to make a difference. You know things, you have passion, and you can help. Don't deny the world your great talents! If you feel nervous, it only means that you care and you really want to do well. The other people in the room want you to do well too.

Board work is already quite simple if you remember the four S's:

📅 **Show Up**

🔊 **Speak Up**

✦ **Shine Up**

🤫 **Shut Up**

SHOW UP

Always show up. Get every meeting on your schedule as soon as they are announced. Schedule all of your other meetings around those meetings. If a client calls, I promise you they can meet you at another time. Your reputation as a team player is on the line. Remember that you committed to them, and when you get there, be there early because on time is late. Be respectful of the time of all of the other members of the board by being ready to get to work.

SPEAK UP

Nothing is worse than a board member who says nothing the entire meeting. You were asked to be on a board so you could contribute. Ask clarifying questions, ask general questions, congratulate the team, and offer some thoughts in your area of expertise.

SHINE UP

Boards are a great opportunity to elevate yourself. Meet all the members; they could be future champions. Agree to serve on committees in areas where you can learn something or flex your talents and contribute. Being on a board is a moment to polish your bio or resume. Be utterly delightful, helpful, and professional.

SHUT UP

Listen. Everyone wants their voice to be heard, so listen to what is being said and be strategic in responding if needed. Listening to the other members of the board is the utmost respect given, and expect a rebound[125] in that respect. While you are listening, log a few questions or notes in that notebook I told you to have about things that you want to discuss, so you don't forget them. Your phone works, too, but the optics are that you are answering emails and not participating in the meeting. When there is a pause, ask those questions. Interrupting may be necessary, but patience is a better strategy.

There are poorly run meetings that could have been emails or meetings that you didn't think you needed to be in. To improve the experience, ask for the agenda ahead of time. You can preplan your actions, knowing what will be covered. Again, if you were asked to be in the meeting, you are needed and you should go to be more informed about the organization that you are representing, even if you are unsure about some of the topics. Learning a new thing is a great gift to yourself, and the bonus to going is that it may be an opportunity to shine your superpowers again. Be strategic with your meetings to gather the information you need to work better, offer suggestions from your perspective, and contribute in a way that helps the entire team.

---

[125] *A rebound in basketball is when a player or team regains possession of the ball after a missed shot. Hey, now everyone is listening to you!*

HUDDLE One area where women fall short is getting or acknowledging their leadership skills. You may think it is safer to do assists,[126] but you know and I know that when it comes to leading, presenting, and getting stuff done, we can do just as well or better than anyone else. If you are still a little squeamish about stepping up, here are things you can do to improve your skills and increase your confidence:

- *Find a book on being a leader.* There are many to choose from and thank you for making this book one of your choices, but others that I have read are *Good to Great* by Jim Collins, *Leaders Eat Last* by Simon Sinek, *The 7 Habits of Highly Effective People* by Stephen Covey, *Dare to Lead* by Brené Brown, and *The 9 Types of Leadership* by Beatrice Chestnut. If this book doesn't give you everything you need, seek out one of these or ask other business leaders what they are reading. Hey, that could be a great conversation starter! Choose the audio version of a book if you comprehend information better when you listen to it.

- *Follow the leader.* Hang around with natural-born leaders and figure out what they do and how they do it. Feel their aura, mimic their style, ask them to lunch, or ask if they could mentor you.

- *Take a course.* This could be as simple as finding many YouTube videos on leadership, or it could also be webinars provided by your work or another organization.

---

[126] *A pass by a player that facilitates a score by another.*

- *Hire a coach.* Sometimes, talent alone can't make you competitive, and you need a coach to help you learn what you need to know to work at a higher level. This could include strategy, pep talks, and mild unprofessional therapy. It is coaching just like any other that helps you practice to be ready for the game.

RULE #9: YOU ARE WORTHY OF TROPHIES AND AWARDS

The potential for greatness lives within each of us.

—Wilma Rudolph, international track and field star and at the height of her career, "the fastest woman in the world"

I categorized myself at a young age as someone who simply does not win things. I competed in a few things and, at best, came in second, but in hindsight, I was still discovering what my strengths were. I did not win the lottery of being born into money, but I did attend the "school of hard knocks" which can be winning in a different way. This also meant that if I wanted anything more than I was handed, I had to strategize a way to get it.

In the discovery period of my life, at about age twelve, I decided that I could take a try at a national drawing contest, the first prize being a new Schwinn ten-speed bike. I knew I was good at drawing so I followed the instructions and let fate take it from there. I won. At that moment, any honorable mentions I had received before just fell away.

The lesson is that if you are good at something or have a passion for it, keep trying things. Many women with fast-growing businesses, or those women who have done something exemplary in their business, just wait for the accolades rather than take the initiative themselves. The truth is that you have to sometimes do the heavy lifting yourself.

In this example of the drawing contest, I did not wait for someone to see the contest and insist that I draw a picture to compete, and then lovingly mail it to the judges. I read about the contest on the back of a cereal box, drew a picture that I was proud of, asked my mom for a large envelope, packed the picture with cardboard so it wouldn't get crushed, and sent it off. Sometimes, we have to take the shot.[127] Sometimes, the spectators are yelling "NO!" because they don't believe that you can do it. They do not see the opportunity, but you do.

When I owned a business, just like the drawing contest, I saw a call for nominations for the fastest-growing businesses in the city. Out of curiosity, I looked at my company's financials to see if we could be a contender. The numbers fit the requirement reflecting continued growth, so we filled out the form and waited to see what happened.

---

[127] *When you have an open opportunity to score in a game.*

We were officially awarded one of the Top 50 Fastest-Growing Businesses. We won that award four more times. We branched out and put our name in for the Inc. 500-5000 Fastest Growing Companies list, because, why not? The first year we made the Inc. 500 list, and we made it four more times on the Inc. 5000 list.

I have heard a number of excuses from women, specifically, as to why they will not seek awards.

- *"No one nominated me."*
- *"I don't have time to fill out the application."*
- *"I don't think I would win."*
- *"There are better people (or companies) out there."*
- *"I was taught to be humble."*
- *"I don't like the spotlight."*
- *"I don't want to share my finances."*

Here is my argument for each of these:

- **No one nominated me.** *A number of award nomination forms only need a contact person from the business. Some need a person to nominate you. People are busy, so if you need someone to nominate you, make it easy for them and ask them if you could use their name as the person nominating you and you will fill out the form. Most of the information is not at the nominator's fingertips, as they will probably not know what your revenue was for the last three years or how happy your employees are. Your champion or cheerleader would be more than happy to offer up their name to fill in the box of who is nominating you for this honor.*
- **I don't have time to fill out the application.** *Applications can be time-consuming, so you will need to make time to do them. Once you have collected a lot of the information, it is easy to find for the next application.*

*Maybe see if there is another one you can fill out now
too. Set aside the time, even if it is thirty minutes a day.
If this were a big client contract, you would find the
time. This small investment of time could lead to more
clients.*

- *I don't think I would win. But you could win. And you
will never win if you don't try.*

- *There are better people (and companies) out there. You
might be surprised. Leadership and numbers are not
always what they appear to be on the outside. Also,
when you are a small, growing company, that is the
prime time to apply for growth awards and recognitions.
Larger companies may experience million-dollar growth,
but the criteria for a lot of these is the percentage of
growth. Did you double your numbers from last year,
for example? Large companies will not double their
revenue, and that gives you an opportunity to shine.
Be aware that a number of the organizations doing
these recognitions love it when there are diverse faces
and different faces every year. It will not factor into
growth recognition, but it could be for leadership. And
before you think a woman might be chosen over a man
just because she is a woman, it is more about women
holding back, and they are actually more qualified for
the recognition.*

- *I was taught to be humble. There is being humble,
and there is leaving money on the table. Anytime
you hold back, you do not present yourself as a solid,
dependable business or as the strong leader you are.
You are sabotaging your own business. Think about it.
If you don't have faith in yourself, others will not either.
Often, those award lists are filled with the names of men
and male-owned businesses because being humble does
not make sense for them. They are looking at facts, not*

feelings. *If you have a solid business, you need to at least try to see if you can get your woman-owned business on that list. Holding back will never get you where you want to go, but it will let you build a more profitable business.*

- *I don't like the spotlight. You will not be followed around by paparazzi for winning these kinds of awards, I promise. But what it will do is open doors for you because this is free press as the company or organization handing out the awards will promote the winners. You get to add to all of your own advertising and media that you are an award-winning company. You get categorized with the other great business leaders. Clients prefer working with a company that has a proven track record, stability, and quality leadership, and has been tried by others with successful results. People like winners, and the winners are not lurking in the shadows.*

- *I don't want to share my finances. Think about why you feel that way. For a lot of people, money has always been treated as a private matter; it most likely started when people remained quiet about their salaries. This is different. This is proof that you are a great leader. This is documentation that you run a strong business. This is your opportunity to be rewarded for your hard work and shout from the rooftops that you are open for business. Men are never afraid to let people know about the success of their business, and women tend to hold back. The result is that they grow their business, buy another business, and sell their business unapologetically. Be brave, be bold, and own your accomplishments. Try not to fear your villains and saboteurs. They will always be there, and they will always play the victim. It is your choice if you are going to let them keep you humble and small. Most, not all, judges need your financials as proof of growth, and they are sworn to secrecy, so all of your information would be safe.*

Let the judges be the judge.

WHISTLE! There will be times when you will fall short of being recognized, or in other words, you lost or didn't make the list. Awards for business growth are a numbers game, and if your growth numbers beat the others, you make the list. It's simple math. You are doing great things; now people know about you and your company. You are also starting to build your legacy. Think about it. After ten or more years of building a business, you can be in the record books forever as a great leader. That acknowledgement makes you a role model for other women, young girls, and even your own children. You don't have the numbers yet? Look into recognitions for Best Places to Work or Most Innovative, awards based on charitable involvement, awards for women-owned specific companies, awards for leadership, etc.

Still don't think that it matters? Think about looking for a place to eat; one place is award-winning, and then there is the other one. Which sounds more desirable? Awards are investments in your own future and the future of your business. Most of all, celebrate the wins by doing something for yourself or your team if it applies. Awards and recognitions are a big deal and deserve a few minutes of reflection, celebration, or treating yourself to that extra spa treatment.

RULE #10: PRACTICE MAKES PERFECT

Champions keep playing until they get it right.

—Billie Jean King, American #1 tennis player, member of the victorious
United States team in seven Federation Cups and nine Wightman Cups. She
also made history playing and beating tennis pro Bobby Riggs in "The Battle
of the Sexes."

Getting on the podium or reaching championship
status does not happen because you tried it once
and had complete success. No one is so lucky that
they fall into success either. This all comes with
practice. But if you make it a part of who you are,
the process gets more manageable, and mountains move. It's
about getting comfortable with the nervousness. It is about
becoming a recovering introvert, if you are one.

By the way, if you are an introvert, just make yourself a mental list of everything you need to accomplish in a gathering. Once you hit that goal, you get to leave. Practice exercising that tolerance of people and get better at it. For me, I am fully aware that people take my energy. Extroverts feed on other people's energy. Know yourself. I would not categorize myself as an introvert, but I know that I have an energy limit and pace myself accordingly. For example, two big gatherings a week are perfect for my energy; anything more, I start to feel the drain. Pace yourself. Keep a cadence, and strike when you know you are at your best. Do you have a one-hour limit? Then make it the most productive hour you can.

So many people quit when they are on the verge of a breakthrough. Keep going, keep learning, keep trying. Your goal is to practice every day to be a C.H.A.M.P.

What is being a C.H.A.M.P? It is practicing these things over and over:

Courage to Show Up

Hustle to Build Your Personal Brand

Act with Boldness

Mentor and Be Mentored (Meaningful Relationships)

Play for Your Legacy

COURAGE TO SHOW UP

Nothing happens if you fail to show up. You may be the queen of excuses, the ultimate introvert, or damaged by fear, but nothing happens if you don't show up. This is how we tackle[128] this:

- *Make a conscious effort to look for the places you need to be. Be selective. Where are your cheerleaders and champions going? Check the websites of organizations of interest; they should have a list of events. Subscribe to e-newsletters from organizations so you are up-to-date on events or gatherings. Ask people you admire where they go for connections. Some to consider would be events with your local Chamber of Commerce and the Chamber of Commerce for the closest large city to you. See if you have a chapter near you for the National Association of Women Business Owners (NAWBO), Women President's Organization (WPO), Entrepreneur's Association (EO), Vistage, and any other organization that will give you opportunities to meet other people in business.*

- *Put those events on your calendar. If you have children or elders to care for, here is my scheduling tip—schedule everything during the day, from events to a meeting at the office, as those can be full of game-changers. Be selective and determine where your ideal client might hang out or where "future you" needs to be seen. It can all happen during the day. I started my business two years before having a child, so I arranged and went to a lot of events during the day while my child was in daycare and school. After-work events happen all of the time, too, so take advantage of those when you*

---

[128] *To try to take the ball from a player on the other team to stop their forward movement by taking hold of the player and making them fall. We just want the ball back.*

*can. Full disclosure: My young child may have made
an appearance at a few of those events. Use your best
judgment.*

- **Sign up, block your calendar, and go to big events.** *This
is your time to grow, and it is an important commitment
you have made to yourself. If you are still choosing
to play small, think about who would benefit if you
chose to play big. You can cover a lot of ground at big
events, so from a numbers standpoint, you can be very
productive.*

- **You might be nervous before any event or meeting.**
*The good news is that this is natural. Everyone gets
nervous because we don't know what to expect. Or is it
excitement? The difference with great leadership is that
you are nervous and you do it anyway. With practice,
this starts to feel comfortable and you begin to show up,
owning the superstar that you are.*

- **Make good choices in what to wear, get the hair on
point, stand tall, take a deep breath, and walk in.**

Showing up is the biggest step. We have countless reasons
not to go, yet going is the thing that makes things happen.

HUSTLE TO BUILD YOUR PERSONAL BRAND

The most effective part of building my personal brand was
to be recognized. The best compliments that you can get are
"I see you everywhere," or "I recognize you from somewhere."
The truth is, I wasn't everywhere, but I was everywhere
I needed to be. People like to recognize other people in a
crowd, and chances are, I was the effervescent, welcoming
event-goer who looked pretty much the same every time. I

approached people with an interest in them and the reason for the event, looking to elevate or help others as I could.

Compare that to someone that bulldozes in and simply is there to take from the room, someone that is not there to build community and elevate all ships. Or someone that is there is complaining to people they don't know, laying their heavy burden on others. I have met all of these types of people, and I am not sorry when I leave the conversation.

As far as carrying your brand, people like working with and knowing people who are predictable, recognizable, and whose reputations are well-known. Think about McDonald's French fries and the comfort we have in how predictable those fries will taste no matter where we are in the world. I didn't have as large of a company by any means, but people knew what they were getting from me. I am giving more than I am taking, I am happier to help or make a connection than close a deal, and overall, I know my stuff. All of this helped to elevate my company brand and my personal brand. This allows for elevation in your community and beyond. You and your brand will be one that people can trust and rely upon. Then, the revenue will start to generate.

ACT WITH BOLDNESS

Always be comfortable with who you are and what you have accomplished. You are in an elite group of women who are doing amazing things. Remember those stats about women in business? You not only belong in this room but everyone needs to know that you are in this room. Walk in with the confidence of the unicorn that you are, because you are not only a leader but you have trained for this.

Remember to get settled, grab a coffee or a snack, and start greeting everyone with a "Hello" or "Hello, how are you?" You will be more memorable, and it will be greatly appreciated if you make people feel welcome, even if you did not call this meeting. So introduce yourself, and if necessary, reintroduce yourself.

Focus on trying to connect with everyone in the room, making sure that you are a good listener first. See if commonalities arise for a great connection. Greet people at all levels because you never know when there is a person in the room who is going to rise to the top. They will remember your kindness.

MENTOR OR BE MENTORED

When in any room, look for the people who are higher on the ladder than you. Don't just look at the women for mentorship, as there are many men who are honored to be the mentor or champion for women. Start like I did, just observing how leaders handle themselves, how they interrupt conversations and "get the ball," how they work the room, etc. It is a constant study of human activity, and it plays out every day, so learn from it as it is the most subtle way to be mentored.

If everyone is dressed to a certain level of professionalism, do the same. The body language and communication are not as dramatic as coaches giving signals[129] to their pitcher or quarterback, but they are there. This comes in handy when knowing when to approach people with experience. I say this because there are times when you can walk up to someone with your playbook in full activation, and someone will give you the vibe that they do not want to be talked to. Be a pro at taking the signals, as it will save you heartache in the long run. If they see me coming and I get the signal, I quickly divert into saying something that needs no response.

- *"Great job."*
- *"Good to see you."*
- *"Love the tie."*
- *"Love the shoes."*
- *Or in Ohio we say, "Go Bucks." It applies to everything.*

On the flipside, if you are at an event and you see a wallflower or rookie,[130] invite them to join you. You never know who they know, and while their career grows, they will remember you. Introduce them to the heavy-hitters[131] that you know in the room. You can teach them what you know or be bold together. Reaching back to help others not only elevates you in the community's perception of you but also offers you a lot of learning and additional connections. I am greatly appreciative of the women and men who welcomed

---

[129] *Coaches give signs using a combination of hand signals and gestures, for example, to convey plays, strategies, and instructions.*

[130] *A person new to an occupation, profession, or hobby. In sports, a rookie is a professional athlete in their first season. We need to watch out for these newbies.*

[131] *A baseball player who hits many home runs and other extra-base hits. In this case, a very important or influential person.*

me into the room. It was a game-changer.[132] When you are in your journey far enough to start to help others, you really start your elevation to legendary status.

---

[132] *An event, idea, or procedure that affects a significant shift in the current manner of doing or thinking about something.*

BE THE LEGEND

My motto has always been that you can't say, 'Oh, it won't happen to me.' You have to say, 'That can happen to me.' So always be aware that things can happen.

—Venus Williams, former world No. 1 tennis champion in singles and doubles, winning seven Grand Slam singles titles and securing four Olympic gold medals

What do I mean when I say, "Be the legend"? Am I saying that you get a hospital wing named after you, maybe a statue erected in your honor? Maybe, because that would be a very great goal,[133] and honestly, why not aim that high? It can happen to you. The only way to even know if this is your legendary mark is to determine what that definition is for you.

_____

[133] *It's a fundamental element in many sports, dictating how teams accumulate points and ultimately determine the winner.*

Much like in the introduction of this book when I asked what your definition of happiness was, I am now asking what is it that you want to be remembered for. There are many, many levels of "legend" that are really quite amazing, and a great place to start is to define what "legendary" means to you. The definition is simply someone who is famous, admired, or spoken about highly. It means that you have left a mark, you have changed the direction for a purpose or a person. You will be remembered. It doesn't mean that you get a scepter or crown, but hey, if someone is offering, take it.

Because you are in a small, elite group of exceptional women, it is to your benefit and the benefit of every woman following you that you push for this. The women around us and those who come after us need to see that anything is possible. You want to achieve your level of legend so when you leave this earth, people will speak highly of you and tell stories about the people you helped. Legendary status is making all of the struggles of your ancestors worth it and makes all future generations proud of you.

Making a mark for yourself or making a difference in the world is also the best gift you can give yourself. All of your work that you have put in over the years and sacrifices that you made were worth it, and you can leave this life satisfied. Anything less is saying that you are okay with being forgotten, and that is not going to happen because there is a plan.

WE NEED TO REALLY SEE SUCCESS FOR OURSELVES FIRST

I thought that cutting paper and gluing pictures to a board was pointless, so it was something that I resisted for years, even if it was defined as a "vision board" when it came to business. What stopped my resistance was when I told a mentor that I did not have a vision board. They immediately asked me, "Well then, how do you know where you are going?" Great question.

The only plan I had was to work harder than I did the day before, hoping that all of those hours would add up to some brilliant kind of success. That is the wrong approach. It is also wrong to think that looking at a bunch of pretty pictures will magically make things happen. In order for you to get where you want to go, you need a map. Otherwise, you are just jumping in the car and driving around, which is fun at the beginning, but soon your passengers will ask, "Where are we going?" or "Are we there yet?" The vision board is images of your destination, but your map is plotting the course. So let's start envisioning the life you want—the one you imagine for yourself, the one that the twelve-year-old you would be so proud of, and then plot the course.

HUDDLE Take a moment to think about people who have reached the heights you would like to reach. This is not about whether you think that you are capable of it at this point, but ultimately, where could you imagine yourself? This is blue-sky thinking in that there is no glass ceiling, only blue sky above our heads. The way up is by balloon, plane, or rocket ship, and you get to choose. Those people you thought about were once where you are right now, and they achieved things that allowed them the freedom to do anything. Not thinking about the how yet, think about what it is you want.

Ask yourself, "What could I do if I had nothing stopping me, if I was not afraid to do it or want it?" This dream is all yours. For some, it might be a mansion. For others, it is a beach house. Your dream could be many trips to far-off places or being cozy in your own little home and never having to work again. I challenge you to think bigger. You could have a couple of homes, you could serve on corporate boards, be an influencer, build enough wealth where you never have to worry about money, build enough wealth where you could start a charity, give to a charity, or add a wing to a college or hospital. Remember your money mindset and what could be stopping you. Remember that money is where women fall short because history shows that we make less, make up for child support payments that don't happen, save less as a result, and suffer financially when we can no longer work.

Think about your dreams and start collecting those images. Yes, that vision board again! Elevate your dreams on occasion. This is a living document in that you can make changes at any time; you will often make changes because you will keep achieving goals and adding more dreams. Wait until you experience the delight of tearing a photo off because you have achieved that goal!

Much like everything I have instructed you to do, this needs to be a part of your inner belief. The next step is to plot the course. Write out the steps it will take to get there—big steps, baby steps, all of the steps. Where a lot of vision boards fall short is that you see the destination but fail to plot the course, so we need to create the map. On a long road trip, you determine how far you can drive in a day and make reservations at hotels. You determine your budget and gas stops and the music you will listen to. You make sure that your car is in perfect running order, and you have asked someone to water your plants. Not plotting the course to your destination could leave you stuck on the side of the road. Think about what small things (or big things) you can do today to start your journey. Give yourself deadlines by adding them to your calendar.

> You will achieve great things, but you need to believe that you will. You need to do this; otherwise, why are you doing all of this work? Start living and growing and not just existing and surviving.

I sharpened my skills, drove a little harder, made connections, asked for help, and took chances because I wanted to achieve a big dream, to be remembered for something. The truth of the matter is that life is short, and you have more control than you think to control your destiny. Whether a little impact or a huge impact, you need to plot your course, get involved, look for opportunities, and be remembered for what you can accomplish or how you were the lynchpin to someone else's greatness.

Things change when we change up our personal game because what we have done so far has only gotten us so far. Really study how others did it, not to mimic it but to come up with your own strategy. Read the stories and watch the videos, and you will find that most of us started down the same road, and then something changed.

> **Your legendary status is within your control.**

Luck may exist, but growth happens when we get really sensitive to seeing opportunities and then chase them. That opportunity could be a connection, an invitation, an event, or something else. Learn to be hypersensitive to opportunities.

Don't get hung up on lost opportunities because the timing might not have been right at that particular moment; you may have still been in building mode. But also don't be afraid when an opportunity comes up and you don't feel ready, because if someone has opened a door for you, they believe that you are ready, and you should believe them. Have the faith in yourself to take that step.

THE ULTIMATE GOAL

I decided to add this last section because I have been asked a lot of questions about selling my business. You can have any goal you wish, but for me, it was simply to be able to retire in comfort. Here are a few thoughts on how you can get there.

Very early on, work with a reputable financial advisor and start saving money. Full disclosure: I did start doing this but lost almost all of it in my divorce at age thirty-five. I started again, as it is never too early or too late to start saving.

If you have a business, do not bank on it being a retirement plan. You have no idea if your business will be worth anything when you are ready to retire. The price of your business is based on what others will pay, not what you think it is worth. So while your business is profitable, save. Pay yourself well with no excuses and save lots of money. You can even take small draws out and invest them in yourself.

For me, the time came when I was feeling my purpose shift and I entertained the idea of selling the business. These bullet points are very broad strokes of the process, but all are based on recurring questions that I get and the process and emotion of making the big decision. These are the next steps we took, but please get any and all information about selling from a paid professional.

- *I talked to my financial advisor and asked if I could live the same lifestyle if I closed the doors of my business today. Surprise! The answer was "yes." My saving skills had paid off, but I did put about twenty years into this business, so let's see what we could get out of it.*
- *I worked with a mentor to get my company to a place where it could run without me. A company's value increases if you are not needed. Also, you don't want to hang around long after the sale.*
- *We determined what kind of sale it would be. We talked about an Employee Stock Ownership Plan (ESOP), just*

hanging out as chairs of our own board, or just selling and walking away.

- *We sought out people for our team to make this happen: financial advisors, accountant, banker, lawyer, and a person that handles mergers and acquisitions. Note that you will be writing a lot of checks to get to that big check.*
- *Get comfortable with what the market will bear for your business. It might be worth more or less than you think. Knowing what your retirement plan needs is key to knowing if you are ready to sell. You might need to be in business a few more years to make up any difference.*
- *Read and reread your Letter of Intent (LOI). The dollar amount offered will never go up, but it can go down during due diligence. Having a merger and acquisitions person in our corner was vital to help us navigate the back-and-forth and protect us from a buyer looking for a bargain.*

Another big thing to think about is, what's next? You can look back at that vision board for any undone dreams, but you may have to think again about that purpose. Think about what lights you up and start exploring that path. If you play your cards right, you will be able to retire with legendary status because you rocked the business world and left your mark.

For me, I still have a few passion projects, and I knew that writing this book was one thing that I needed to do. It is my way of letting other women in business see the notes that I took along the way and hopefully get more women in the room and to the top. Your path can operate within your comfort zone, but at minimum, get yourself in a place of peace and comfort. This could involve pushing your own boundaries, and a lot of the tactics are here in this book.

Get in the room, do great things, make money, and be the leader you were born to be.

YOU ARE WHAT CHAMPIONS ARE MADE OF

I don't feel pressure from the outside because the expectations that I put on myself are way greater than what anybody could think or want or have of me.

—Candace Parker, champion basketball player and regarded as one of the greatest WNBA players of all time

For the women (or men) who have read this book and are thinking, "This is all amazing stuff, but I really don't think that I can do it," know that you can. I know this because you want to win; you would not have read my book if you didn't have a tiny feeling that you could do it. And if you haven't pieced it together already, my story did not start as a winning formula. I had to make choices. I had to redirect. I had to take a leap of faith by knowing that the math worked out, because when I started:

I did not come from money.

- *My parents were not business owners.*
- *As a "latchkey" kid, I had to raise my sibling and become very resourceful.*
- *I was taken advantage of by a trusted individual.*
- *I started working at a young age and put myself through college.*
- *An expensive divorce derailed everything. (Divorce is expensive but worth it.)*
- *I hopped around from job to job because I was a bit lost.*

But then ...

- *I stayed focused on a vision of a better life.*
- *I built a great reputation based on my work ethic and caring for others, and stayed connected with people.*
- *With the years of connections I made I had people that believed in me and my starting of a business.*
- *I restructured my personal life, grew that business, and went on to amazing things.*

> **I want you to see that regardless of what life hands you, you can accept it or bat it away. Stay focused on your vision and practice everything you need to reach that goal. Start having the mindset of a champion.**

All is possible when you make big changes in the direction that you want to go. Think of it as getting off that winding, dusty road and getting on the highway. A "what do I do now" moment was my recalibration and mindset change, that moment when I chose to do things differently because I had nothing to lose. It was also the moment when I really became aware of how the game of business is played.

Everything I have instructed you to do is based on how the men are playing the game. Do not get lost in how a lady should behave because men are the ones winning. There are expectations that always echo in our heads, and it is hard to shake them out. Changing direction only happens when we study the playbook and change how we play the game, not just doing more of the same thing. Practice, practice, practice until it is all second nature and people see you walk in with your power. Since you are more powerful after reading this book, let me take you deeper with these four truths of power that will elevate you more:

1. *Women Own Businesses Where They Treat It Like It Is a Job or a Child That They Need to Sacrifice For:* Men pay themselves. Men do not sacrifice their own income because the business is short on cash. They are not afraid of standing firm in their pricing. And there are a few of you that think differently, but a lot of the female business owners that I have met skip paying themselves when times get tough, slash prices in order to get a deal closed and give money away rather than save it for their own futures. I said it, I've seen it, and we need to do better. You are running a business. You are not only the president of your company, but you are also the owner. Imagine if you were only the owner and hired a president to run your company. Now, think about telling your president that they will not be paid

for the next few months because cash flow is slow. This is not good business, and you need to think about how you need to make some big changes in order to keep your business afloat. As the owner, you need to have a great relationship with at least three bankers in case there are money crunches. Open a line of credit before you need the money. Have a solid relationship with a banker that you can call when you need something fast. If they can't do it, call the next banker. Business ownership should be about you growing beyond startup thinking. My thoughts when we opened the business were that if we could not pay ourselves in six months, we would have to close the business. We never closed, and we always paid ourselves. We did tap into that line of credit on occasion to pay people, and quickly paid the company back. This is a business, not your personal bank account; keep them separate. While you are paying yourself from your company funds, always factor in saving money for your retirement. It is not guaranteed that you will have your company until the day you retire. And guess what? It may not be as big of a payday as you think. Always pay yourself or figure out your cash flow problem. Find an advisor you can trust and start saving now.

2. *Self-Promotion and Bragging:* Men in business are often more comfortable with self-promotion, openly discussing their achievements, and showcasing their success.

It is hard to break that mindset when we are conditioned from birth to be nice, be humble, and support others to a fault. I cannot express how much we need women to step up and show other women that owning their success is so important. My pro tip for getting over that hurdle is to just speak to the facts. If you won an award, tell people. Post about it on all of your social media, and if you are still struggling with being humble, say something like, "I am so honored to have been selected as the Most Amazing Woman in America," or "Thank you to Super Cool Company for naming me the Most Amazing Woman in America." It is so easy that I am going to call it a tip-in.[134] Add everything to your bio or resume. Quick reminder: You can initiate those recognitions too. See the earlier chapter about that. If you qualify, apply. Better yet, if you think you almost qualify, apply. Let the judges decide because the men applying are simply taking the shot too.

3. *Taking Risks and Going After Big Opportunities:* Men in business are sometimes more willing to take the big shots—whether it's starting their own business, launching a new product, or making bold decisions. Women tend to operate more cautiously. I have always hated it when people say that entrepreneurs, business owners, and leaders are risk-takers. It may look like

---

[134] *In basketball, a "tip-in" refers to a goal scored by a player deflecting a missed shot, or a ball that has come off the rim and into the basket from very close range, just tapping that baby in with the fingertips.*

that on the outside, but we are all running the numbers over and over in our heads so we don't fail. Where women can step up more is going for the big deals. Do not be afraid of big contracts, big companies, and big opportunities. Don't be afraid because you will figure it out. Have faith that you will find the people, the money, and the infrastructure to make it all happen. Ask for help. There are so many sources for help that anything you try will not be that big of a risk. The people that you need to know for growth are the people you need to be networking with now. Have these people in a position where they will not only take your call, but they will already know most of your business history. Take big leaps and think about regional growth, acquisitions, partnerships, and mergers as a way to grow.

4. *Displaying Confidence Without Apology:* Confidence is often seen as a key to success in business, and men tend to feel more comfortable expressing confidence without fear of judgment. Women, on the other hand, may face challenges with balancing confidence and humility, apologizing constantly, or seeing problems as something that is their fault. Again, stop apologizing for everything. Care for yourself with all of the fire that lights you from within. You will be the person that everyone wants to know or be, and from there, you will become a legend.

These four final thoughts, combined with all of the scripts and coaching in this book, are the things that elevate you to the leader you were born to be. I have never asked you to stop getting your nails done, being gorgeous, or being anything less than you are. I have not said one disparaging remark about men. As a matter of fact, I love them in the room because of the collaboration, their experience, and the fact that they like to get down to business and make some money. They are also easy to work with when we are all speaking the same language and working under all of the same rules.

Life is short. You need to leave a mark and be remembered. It won't be perfect, and that is what makes this life all yours.

On your mark.

Get set.

GO!

THE BOOK REFERENCES

Jill Bolte Taylor, Ph.D., *Whole Brain Living: The Anatomy of Choice and the Four Characters That Drive Our Life*

Brené Brown, *Dare to Lead: Brave Work. Tough Conversations. Whole Hearts; I Thought It Was Just Me (but It Isn't): Making the Journey from "What Will People Think?" to "I Am Enough"*

Gallup and Don Clifton, *StrengthsFinder 2.0*

Simon Sinek, *Find Your Why?; Leaders Eat Last*

Gay Hendricks, *The Big Leap: Conquer Your Hidden Fear and Take Life to the Next Level*

Casey Brown, *Fearless Pricing: Ignite Your Team, Own Your Value, and Command What You Deserve*

Mark A. Williams, PhD, *The Connected Species: How the Evolution of the Human Brain Can Save the World*

Jim Collins, *Good to Great: Why Some Companies Make the Leap...and Others Don't; Great By Choice*

Stephen R. Covey, *The 7 Habits of Highly Effective People*

Beatrice Chestnut, PhD, *The 9 Types of Leadership: Mastering the Art of People in the 21st Century Workplace*

Mark Hensen, *Ordinary Superpowers: Unleash the Full Potential of Your Most Natural Talents*

Richard Schwartz, *No Bad Parts: Healing Trauma & Restoring Wholeness with the Internal Family Systems Model*

Karen Hough, *Be the Best Bad Presenter Ever: Break the Rules, Make Mistakes, and Win Them Over*

Glennon Doyle, *Untamed*

ABOUT THE AUTHOR

Catherine Lang-Cline is a highly accomplished CEO, entrepreneur, and C-Suite executive who brings an innovative vision and design thinking to various sectors, including consumer products and services, financial services, and technology. Catherine has a proven track record in creating high-value business models such as marketplaces and digital platforms and deep expertise in entrepreneurship, strategy, marketing, and human resources. She also brings a deep background in board governance through her extensive experience serving as a board director for non-profit and industry boards.

Catherine is an experienced community and not-for-profit Board Member including: the Columbus College of Art and Design, she served nine years on the Columbus Chamber of Commerce Board and on its Strategy Committee, seven years as a Board Member of the Greater Columbus Art Council, Executive Committee, and Finance Committee. Catherine also served as president/chair of the National Association of Women Business Owners, Columbus Chapter, and its local and national Public Policy Committee.

With 20 years of experience as the CEO of Portfolio Creative, Catherine Lang-Cline is recognized by her peers as a top executive with five consecutive years as Columbus CEO - Most Admired CEO, Most Influential Entrepreneur, Smart Woman - Progressive Entrepreneur Award, Smart 50 Award, Business First Influential Women to Know, Small Business Leader Award - Finalist, NAWBO Visionary Award - Finalist, six years honored as an Inc. 500-5000 Fastest Growing Privately-Owned Companies, WELD "Women You Should Know", Columbus Chamber Entrepreneur of the Year, Business First Best Temporary Employment Agency, six years awarded the Business First Fast 50, E&Y Entrepreneur of the Year Finalist.

Catherine has 15 years of experience in marketing for Fortune 500 companies and small to mid-sized businesses before starting and scaling her own business in 2005. Catherine contributed her expertise in marketing and design in the category of retail consumer goods, personal products, banking, travel, and more.

As a business leader, public speaker, and thought leader, Catherine is also an expert in entrepreneurship, strategy, marketing, human resources, and culture building, making it possible to assist in large-scale changes within organizations that affect the bottom line. Catherine shares her experience and knowledge in blogs and articles, her podcast *Illumination Bureau*, and *The Secret Art of Business*. She has also been a speaker at The Ohio State University, Keynote - Women's Conference at The OSU Fisher School of Business, The American Staffing Association, and the WSBA Women's Leadership Conference. Catherine held a Staffing Professional Certification with the American Staffing Association for over a decade. She received a Bachelor of Fine Arts Degree from Northern Illinois University, where she was honored as an Alumnus of Achievement.